ENERGY MANAGEMENT: CAN WE LEARN FROM OTHERS?

ENERGY MANAGEMENT: CAN WE LEARN FROM OTHERS?

George F. Ray

Gower

Published by
Gower Publishing Company Limited,
Gower House, Croft Road, Aldershot, Hants GU11 3HR,
England

Gower Publishing Company
Old Post Road, Brookfield, Vermont 05036,
USA

British Library Cataloguing in Publication Data

Ray, George
    Energy management : can we learn from others?——
    (Energy paper; no. 16)
    1. Power resources.
    I. Title   II. Series
    333.79'17   HD9502.A2

    ISBN 0-566-05015-3

Contents

List of Tables

List of Charts

Foreword

The Joint Energy Programme is very grateful for the opportunity to publish this important research paper by Professor George Ray of the National Institute for Economic and Social Research. His analysis of Energy Management in other countries, and his ideas on what the UK can learn from them is a valuable addition to the work which the Joint Energy programme has itself done in the past 18 months on various aspects of UK energy, as detailed below:

Energy Paper No 8:   International Gas Trade in Europe, Jonathan P. Stern

Energy Paper No 9:   Coal's Contribution to UK Self-Sufficiency, Louis Turner

Energy Paper No 10:   Gas's Contribution to UK Self-Sufficiency Jonathan P. Stern

Energy Paper No 11:   Electricity's Contribution to UK Self-Sufficiency, Richard Eden and Nigel Evans

Energy Paper No 12:   Oil's Contribution to UK Self-Sufficiency, Colin Robinson and Eileen Marshall

Energy Paper No 13:   Conservation's Contribution to UK Self-Sufficiency, Mayer Hillman

Energy Paper No 14:   The Economics of Energy Self-Sufficiency, Eileen Marshall and Colin Robinson

In addition Gower will publish in the summer of 1985 a further volume drawing on the information contained in the above, under the title "Energy Self Sufficiency for the UK?". This will constitute a report on the conference of the same name held in the series of Joint Studies in Public Policy in December 1984.

The Joint Energy Programme (JEP) is under the joint auspices of the Policy Studies Institute and the Royal Institute of International Affairs. It conducts research into national and international energy policy questions. However the views and interpretations presented in its publications are those of the authors and not necessarily those of the institutions concerned.

We hope that this series of papers will make a contribution to public debate on energy issues and to the development of policy by government and industry.

Robert Belgrave
March 1985

Acknowledgements

This study was carried out at the National Institute of Economic and Social Research, supported by a grant from the Leverhulme Trust, whose assistance is gratefully acknowledged.

Dr David Jones of the International Energy Agency in Paris and Professor Colin Robinson of the University of Surrey in Guildford were particularly helpful in giving advice and information as well as in commenting on a previous draft of this paper; thanks are due to them for their willing assistance. Naturally, they are in no way responsible for the contents of this study.

I also wish to thank my colleagues at the National Institute for their help during the course of the work, particularly the Secretary of the Institute, Mrs K Jones, for managing the financial and many other aspects of the project; Mrs F Robinson for her help in editing this final report; and Mrs R Charlton for her patient and invaluable secretarial assistance.

George F Ray

Introduction

Following the 1973 and 1979-80 'oil shock' the question of how to maintain a secure energy supply has come to the fore in every country, advanced or developing, centrally planning or with a market economy. After the haphazard measures taken under pressure of physical scarcity in 1973-4, many countries have formulated longer term plans with major programmes of varying degrees of sophistication which embrace their whole 'energy economy'. These have been modified and altered, some of them several times, in the light of the changing world energy situation.

This change has been spectacular and dramatic. In the space of ten years the world energy situation has pivoted from scarcity to oversupply, from a seller's market to a buyer's. Most students of the energy scene agree, however, that the present glut is likely to be temporary. The International Energy Agency, instituted soon after the first oil shock, continuously warns in its various publications of the danger of complacency. A recent study [1] concluded that, 'the combination of moderate income and oil price assumptions points to an increasing pressure on the world oil balance in the 1990s' but 'if oil prices decline in real terms in the 1983-90 period, world oil demand may further increase' and this means that 'pressure on prices may come much earlier depending on OPEC's ability to hold a ceiling on its combined oil output'.

All this gives rise to several major uncertainties. First, whilst it is beyond doubt that a good deal of the reduction in demand for energy must have been due to the prolonged recession/stagnation in the world economy, which more truly characterised the decade after the first oil shock than the short-lived and relatively weak upswings, it still remains to be seen how demand will develop in a period of sustained recovery. Secondly, it is difficult to assess the ability of the main oil producers, perhaps not so much their physical capability as the combination of the many factors that they presumably take into account when production targets are set and the uncertainty surrounding the observation of these targets. We need to know also the production potential of energy importers and the outcome of the general endeavour aimed at the more rational, productive and efficient use of energy, with its objective of switching from a relatively scarce to a relatively more abundant source of energy, in fact all that has now come to be referred to as 'energy conservation'. Finally, public debate on the environmental impact of different forms of energy (particularly, but not exclusively, coal burning) and continuing doubts about the safety of nuclear power may lead to tighter controls which could themselves become important supply side constraints. Application of recently developed theories of the school of rational expectation also adds to the uncertainties. As long as the future looked bright, public or private investors, optimistic of rising fuel prices, made ambitious plans, backed up by the promise of an uninterrupted upsurge of energy prices, which boosted investment appraisals and helped to overcome that degree of risk which is unavoidably attached to projects with a long gestation period, a particular feature of major energy investments. In the 1970s, such expectations might have seemed rational. With time, however, the situation has changed significantly: energy prices, particularly in real terms but also nominally, have taken a sharp downward turn. Rational expectation required the revision, in the same direction, of many major investment plans (the US synthetic fuel projects being a case in point) and might have affected, on a micro level, the conservation investments of many energy users as well.

The dichotomy between national and private interests further complicates matters as the movement in prices of primary energy (the cost to the national import bill) and of fuels in final use (what consumers eventually pay) has not been parallel. For a long time, and to some extent even now, the rise in the cost of fuel consumption lagged behind that of imported energy,[2] thus negatively influencing consumers' investment decisions in the conservation area (through long payback) in relation to the 'national interest'. There are, of course, other areas where public and private interests diverge, for example in the context of the security of supply or the environmental impact of energy.

Various countries have approached all these problems and uncertainties in different ways, and have achieved different results. The objective of this study can be summed up very briefly: what can be learnt from their plans, programmes and experiences that may be of use in formulating UK energy policy?

At present there is no comprehensive and accepted energy policy in the UK. There are various piecemeal decisions, announcements of intentions and plans, which together form an approach to energy management of a sort. Given the UK's fortunate position of being, for the moment, abundantly supplied with domestic energy resources, this may be understandable. Given also, however, the limited lifetime of two major sources of energy, North Sea oil and gas, this happy situation cannot last long. Before the end of the century, and possibly much earlier, the UK will again become an energy importer on a considerable scale; a more specific approach, therefore, to the management of the country's energy economy (as well as to allied problems that will emerge in related sectors) will then be desirable, even if the government of the day may in general prefer to take a non-interventionalist stance.

The following question is thus topical, if not yet urgent: what can we learn from other countries, particularly from those presently less well endowed with domestic energy resources than the UK is now?

THE SCOPE AND STRUCTURE OF THIS STUDY
Energy plans/programmes and, in a wider sense, the energy situation, in a total of 33 countries, have been studied, covering sixteen European and five non European OECD countries, two centrally planned economies and ten selected developing countries. Abstracts of their energy situations and plans are summarised briefly in the appendix.

On the basis of surveying these national approaches quite a few general points are made and the assessment which follows shows the major differences that tend to determine energy policies in some of the larger countries - and in some of the more interesting of the remainder.

The next step was to assess the success, or otherwise, of energy management in these countries, here restricted to the advanced market economies, that is the OECD countries. This part of the exercise was carried out with two aims in mind: first to obtain a picture, both by country and overall, of the relationship between national output and energy use; and secondly, to serve as a basis for selecting the most 'successful' countries, which could then be subjected to more thorough analysis.

Various aspects of energy economy and management are now picked out in order to point to departures in some areas which may warrant consideration. In many respects other countries follow in principle the same practices as the UK (tax incentives, for example) and in these cases there are few differences worth noting. Other aspects deserve more detailed treatment however. Whilst the differences between approaches to broaden the domestic energy base are larger and wider ranging than those affecting the demand side (in particular conservation), they depend to some extent on the natural endowment of each country and those with little relevance to the UK are not mentioned at length.

SOME GENERAL POINTS

The success, or otherwise, of policy measures can be assessed in one way only; by their effect. However, as will be discussed in some detail later on, attributing effects to policies, or to one single policy measure among often quite a basketful of them, is always problematic and frequently impossible, usually because of the lack of information.

The difficulty lies not only in separating out the effect of one specific measure from that of other measures but also in assessing whether the differences among countries are due to policy or other factors, such as differences in political, social and economic conditions. (For instance, the effects of government legislation/regulation, on the one hand, and exhortation/recommendation on the other, can vary greatly; a recommendation by MITI in Japan may well have stronger effects than a law in some other countries.)

The strong tendency to 'conserve' energy in general, and oil in particular, in nearly all countries suggests that fuel price increases have had a very significant effect. The extent to which governments have allowed energy price increases to be passed on to the final fuel consumers and the effects of the exchange rate variations on the cost of imported energy have been important (as well as other specific policy measures). Thus, although a detailed analysis of energy pricing in the various countries was not possible within the scope of this study, the important role of prices should be stressed: pricing policies seem crucial especially for countries which rely primarily on market forces to bring about a healthy energy mix and improve energy efficiency.

It is also necessary to point out that the extent to which policies result in energy-saving or energy-switching does not, or not necessarily, measure (or even reflect) their overall cost effectiveness.

Despite these shortcomings, some interesting points, as well as some generally useful experiences, have been gathered together in the course of this study so that we may be able to benefit from our knowledge of other countries' practices.

DIFFERENT APPROACHES TO ENERGY POLICY

Each of the countries covered in this enquiry is in a particular situation, unique to itself. Its approach to energy policy is determined by its own natural resources and by historical factors which have shaped consumer behaviour.

Whilst the energy policy of the United Kingdom is clearly influenced by the country's present wealth of energy resources and the present government's belief that, in general, market forces are the most effective method of regulating the market and allocating resources in the energy sector, other countries in less fortunate resource positions are following different paths.

France, for example, has embarked on the development of a powerful nuclear power industry, supported by a strong conservation programme. Belgium has also decided on an ambitious plan with similar features.

German energy policy is characterised by two major factors, the existence of a large and high-cost domestic coal industry which cannot easily be run down, and a reliance on imports for nearly all hydrocarbons. This in turn leads them to put some oil supplies under national control through Deminex, the German exploration company; but otherwise, as in the UK, to rely on market forces to bring about a good energy pattern.

Considerable liberalislation was required in order to allow market forces to help shape the energy scene more efficiently in the United States, where the initial spurt to exploit new resources has recently weakened significantly.

Japanese policy has until recently been dominated by the need for security of supply, given the scarcity of domestic resources. Energetic programmes have thus been introduced aiming at diversifying sources to give a secure long-term supply and at reducing energy use and thereby imports (though now more weight is being given to the balance between energy security and costs).

In other countries again various factors stand out as governing the main lines of departure, such as, for example, the further extension of district heating, with combined heat and power production, in the Nordic countries, particularly Denmark, where a forceful switch to coal helps to reduce reliance on oil.

These few cases, concentrating only on the most characteristic lines of approach, will suffice to illustrate the divergence, determined by the particular situation in each country, in their energy policies.

ENERGY USE IN OECD COUNTRIES

The set of diagrams on chart 1 shows, for the years 1973 to 1983, four main indicators for each of the OECD countries included: gross domestic product, industrial production, primary energy use and oil consumption. Simple optical inspection conveys the impression, even without any further analysis of the data, that in the vast majority of cases primary energy consumption lagged behind national production, and oil consumption even more so (pages 11 and 12).

In most cases the lag of industrial production behind GDP itself suggests falling energy intensity in the national economies, demonstrating the advancing role of the tertiary service sector. This, or at least its many important branches, is relatively less energy demanding than industrial activity. Two further points should be noted in this context. First, the apparently more efficient use of energy reflects not only conservation (in the strict sense) but also structural changes in output, such as the shift away from energy intensive industries, for example iron and steel. Conservation itself comprises various elements, including changes in behaviour; investment in new, more energy-efficient plant; retrofitting; modification of the production process or of the existing equipment, and so on. These cannot be separated at the national level.

Secondly, even after making these relative reductions in the energy use of the countries shown, the import bill on energy remains high for most of them, absorbing a large proportion of their export earnings (table 2).

These data have been further processed and, as a result, chart 2 (page 13) shows the year-to-year development of two indicators in the same period: the energy-GDP and the oil-GDP ratios. The energy-GDP ratio shows, in most cases, considerable relative reduction in energy use in all countries, with the exception of Portugal, Spain and Switzerland, whilst the oil-GDP ratio falls even more in most cases (this time with the sole major exception of Portugal). Table 1 repeats the figures in tabular form for the same countries (page 14).

Using these methods of approach we find that almost all countries in the advanced world have achieved considerable energy saving as related

to their output. They have reduced oil usage to an even larger extent
by means of replacing it with some other form of primary energy. The
latter could only have been achieved in one of two ways: either by
importing more non-oil energy or increasing production of other
domestic energy sources (see table 3). In most market economies,
including developing countries (LDCs), the domestic contribution to
energy supplies has grown since 1973. (For the centrally planned
economies in Eastern Europe, except the USSR, the opposite is true.)

As we have already pointed out, each of our sample countries has some
unique features. Their natural endowments are different, as are their
opportunities for reducing energy use within their own output
structure. Nor is this a kind of Olympic race. Nevertheless, we are
able to obtain a general impression of their achievements in energy
management which then helps us to select a smaller number of countries
whose energy economies are worth closer investigation.

The countries which were selected for this purpose, therefore, are
(in no particular order of achievement): Denmark, France, the
Netherlands, Sweden, Japan, Belgium, Ireland and Norway. These are
advanced countries with an economic structure very crudely comparable
[3] with that of the UK and, in view of their results in the energy
management area, it is believed that a closer study of their practices
deserves attention. There are, of course, other countries in
situations similar to that of the UK, insofar as structure or
historical background is concerned, and they are of no less importance
for having been left out of the above list (Germany is a case in
point). But the limit has to be drawn somewhere. Moreover, in the
sections that follow the brief case studies of these eight selected

10

countries, we will draw on the energy programmes of all 33 countries; thus, if anything particularly noteworthy emerges from any other programme (including for example the German) it will receive mention there.

Chart 1

Output and energy use in OECD countries, 1973-83

1973 = 100

Key: G = GNP or GDP   I = Industrial production

E = Primary energy consumption   O = Oil consumption

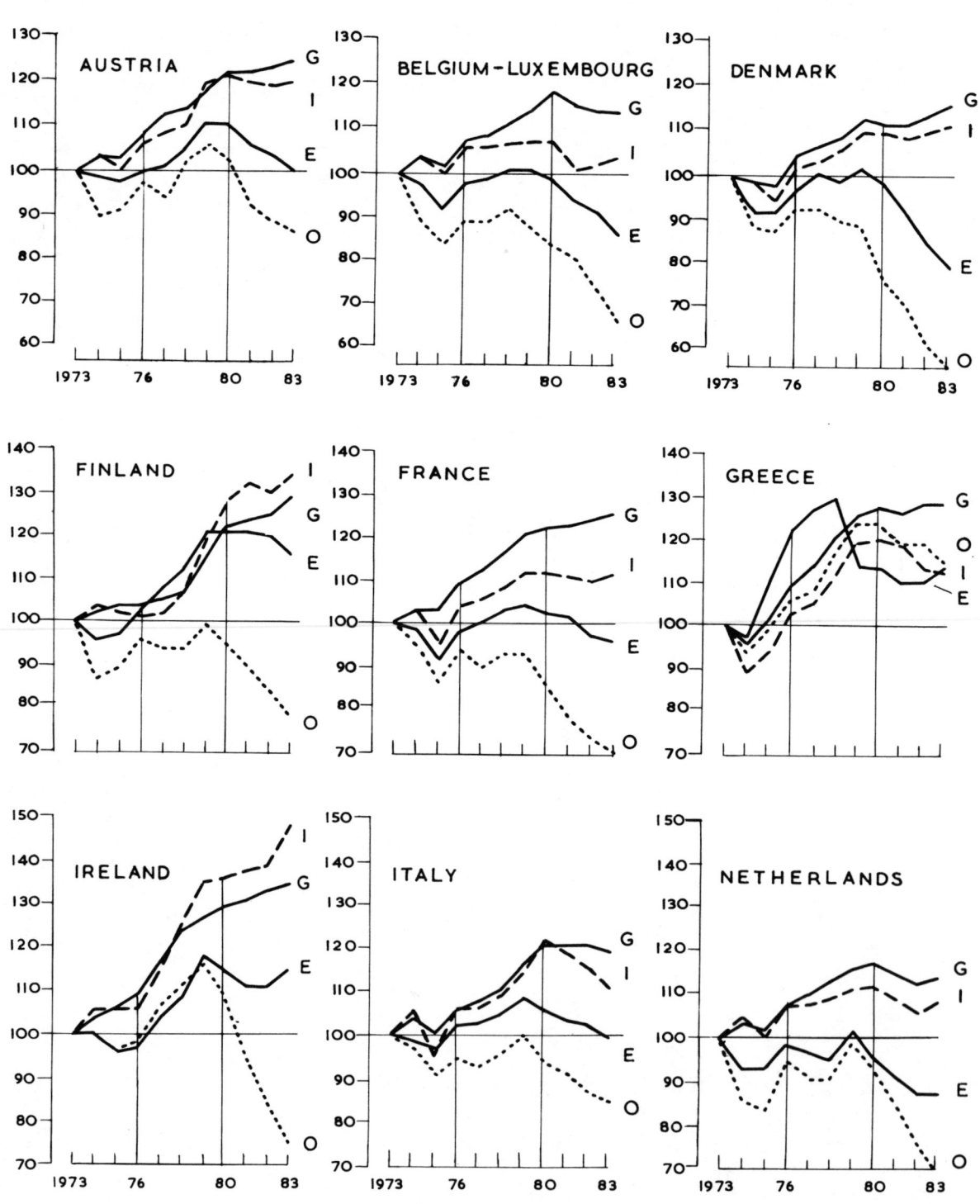

Chart 1

(Continued)

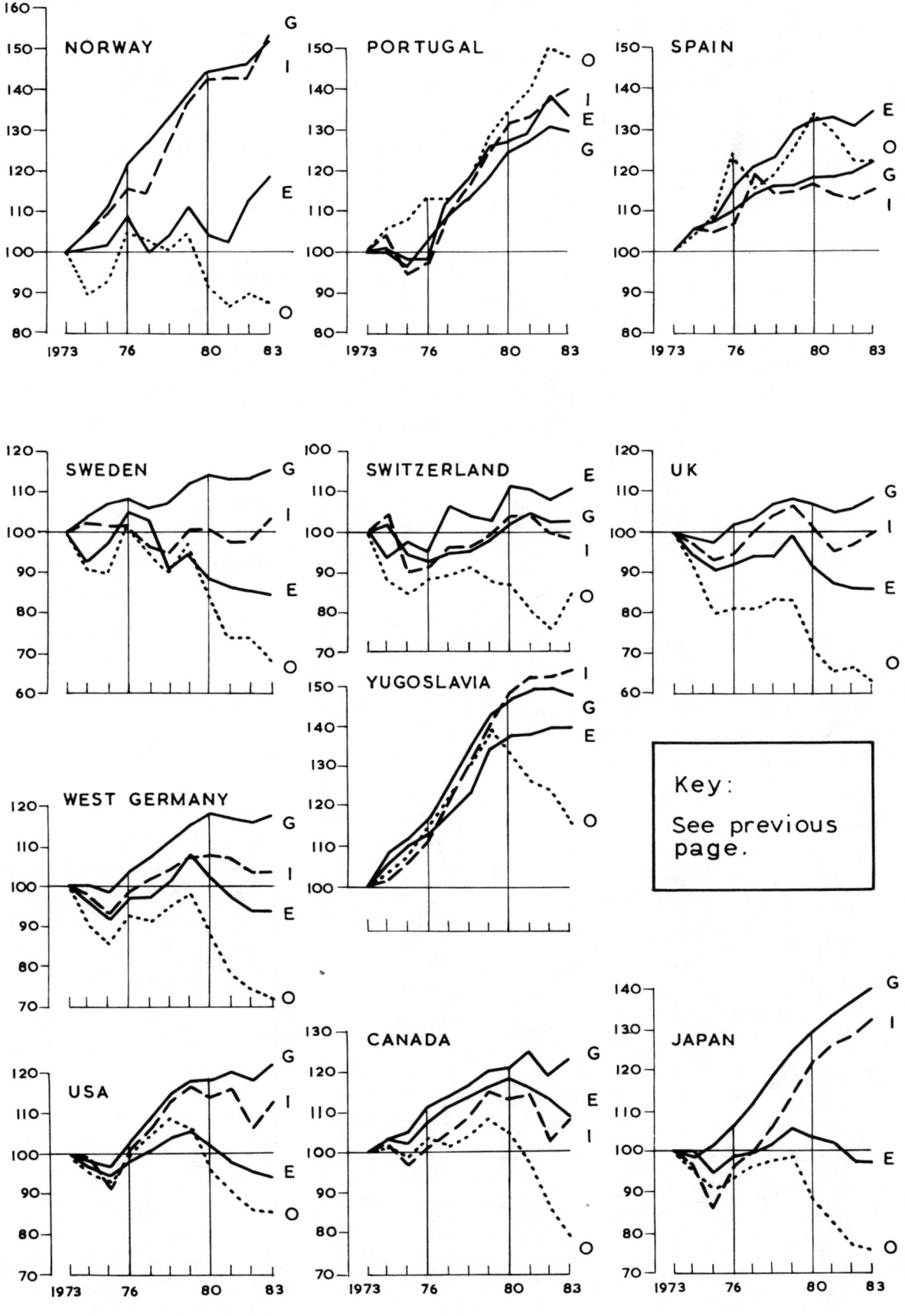

Key:

See previous page.

Chart 2
Primary energy and oil consumption related to GDP
1973 = 100

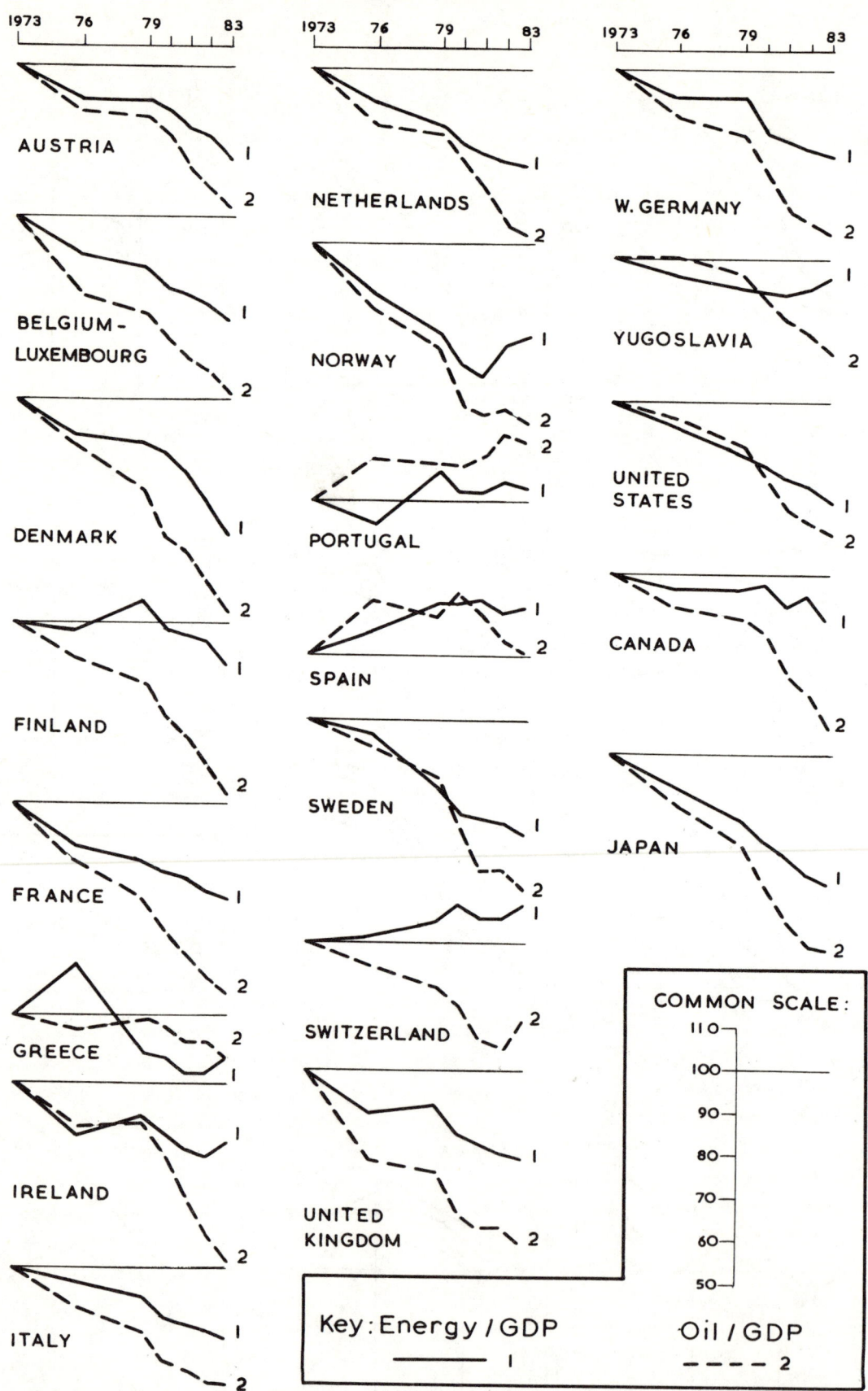

Source for charts 1 and 2: OECD National Accounts, Industrial Production and Main Economic Indicators, BP Statistical Review of World Energy, 1984.

Table 1
Energy and oil consumption related to GDP
1973 = 100

	Primary energy [a]						oil [b]					
	1976	79	80	81	82	83	1976	79	80	81	82	83
Austria	93	93	90	86	84	79	91	89	84	76	72	67
Belgium	91	88	83	82	79	75	82	77	71	67	64	58
Denmark	92	90	88	82	75	66	89	79	68	64	54	50
Finland	99	105	99	98	96	90	92	87	79	74	68	60
France	90	87	84	82	79	78	86	78	70	64	58	56
Greece	112	91	90	87	87	90	97	99	98	94	94	90
Ireland	89	93	89	85	84	86	90	92	84	73	64	58
Italy	97	93	88	86	84	83	90	85	78	76	73	72
Netherlands	92	88	82	80	78	77	88	86	79	75	66	61
Norway	89	80	72	70	77	78	86	76	62	60	61	58
Portugal	95	107	102	102	105	103	110	109	108	110	115	114
Spain	106	112	112	113	110	111	113	109	114	109	103	100
Sweden	97	85	78	77	76	73	94	87	75	65	65	59
Switzerland	102	105	109	106	106	109	95	90	85	78	75	82
UK	90	92	85	83	81	79	79	77	66	63	63	59
W Germany	94	94	86	84	81	80	89	85	75	68	65	62
Yugoslavia	97	94	93	92	93	95	100	97	91	85	83	78
US	95	89	86	83	81	77	97	90	82	76	73	70
Canada	97	97	98	93	95	89	93	90	87	78	73	64
Japan	93	85	80	77	72	70	89	80	68	62	56	54

Source: OECD National accounts, industrial statistics, Main Economic Indicators;
BP statistical review of world energy, 1984.

[a] $100(E_1/E_{73} : GDP_1/GDP_{73})$ [b] $100(O_1/O_{73} : GDP_1/GDP_{73})$

Where E = total primary energy and O = oil consumption.

15

Table 2

OECD countries' energy import bill as percentage of visible export
earnings, 1982 and 1983

| | Per cent of total exports | | |
	1982	1983	Change
Austria	18.5	15.8	+
Belgium/Luxembourg	11.7	(11)*	+
Denmark	21.5	15.3	+
Finland	23.4	22.1	+
France	29.5	23.6	+
Germany FR	17.0	15.8	+
Greece	55.6	(55)*	+
Ireland	17.1	13.2	+
Italy	31.4	29.4	+
Netherlands	0.6	0.5	+
Norway	-40.8	-45.1	+
Sweden	19.3	15.0	+
UK	-6.8	-10.1	+
Canada	-6.6	-8.4	+
US	24.8	24.2	+
Japan	47.2	39.8	+

Source: OCED Trade Statistics, Series A (monthly), May-June, 1984.
Notes: The figures show the net imports (imports less exports) of
        energy (SITC section 3) as a percentage of the country's total
        visible exports both expressed in US dollars.

        Data for countries not shown are not available in a comparable
        form.
        Invisible trade excluded.
        Figures marked by an * are provisional estimates.
        A minus sign indicates net exports.

A + sign in the 'Change' column indicates improvement: either smaller
net imports or higher net exports.

Table 3

The share of domestic production in total primary

energy consumption, [a] 1973-1982

	1973 per cent	1982	change			1973 per cent	1982	change
1) OECD-EUROPE					**3) CENTRALLY PLANNED**			
Austria	38	32	–		Bulgaria	41	36	–
Belgium	15	16	+		Czechoslov.	75	69	–
Denmark	½	10	+		East Germany	74	73	–
Finland	6	18	+		Hungary	63	56	–
France	22	26	+		*Poland	114	105	–
Germany FR	48	48	=		Romania	101	89	–
Greece	19	35	+		*USSR	121	129	+
Ireland	14	38	+		Yugoslavia	68	66	–
Italy	17	18	+		**4) SELECTED LDC'S**			
Luxembourg	2	1	–					
*Netherlands	78	110	+		*Argentina	92	112	+
*Norway	60	331	+		Brazil	36	48	+
					Chile	54	64	+
Portugal	13	8	–					
Spain	24	29	+		*Egypt	133	197	+
Sweden	16	28	+		Ghana	32	45	+
					Ivory Coast	2	51	+
Switzerland	18	28	+					
*United Kingdom	54	123	+		India	81	92	+
					*Indonesia	550	330	–
2) OTHER OECD					Kenya	3	10	+
*Australia	131	142	+		Pakistan	62	69	+
*Canada	133	115	–		Sri Lanka	5	11	+
Japan	9	11	+		Thailand	3	16	+
New Zealand	44	70	+					
USA	85	91	+					

	OECD	CP	LDC	TOTAL
+	17	1	11	29
–	4	7	1	12
=	1	0	0	1
Total	22	8	12	42

Source: UN Yearbook of World Energy Statistics, 1982.
* Denotes net energy exporters in 1981.
[a] Commercial energy only. Stock changes disregarded.

The Energy Situation in the Selected Countries

DENMARK

In 1973, Denmark's energy imports accounted for nearly 100 per cent of requirements. With no more than 5-6 per cent of primary energy needs met by domestic sources the Danes had the highest level of import dependence in Western Europe. After the 1979 oil price rise energy imports absorbed one fifth of all export earnings.

The approach to the problem did not differ much from the measures taken in many other countries - fuel substitution, conservation and energy resource development - but the objectives have been powerfully and consistently supported by subsequent governments. Indeed, current legislation on the 'Danish Heat Plan' requires intensive government intervention on central and local levels. Thus, whilst there was not much difference in kind betwen the Danish approach and that of other countries, the difference in degree was considerable. The two pillars of the policy for reducing dependence on oil were substitution and the promotion of the production and use of natural gas.

The immediate route to fuel substitution required a rapid increase in the use of imported coal. Since 1973, coal's share in primary supplies, as well as the absolute quantity, has risen spectacularly. This was largely, though not exclusively, due to the conversion of oil-fired power plants. In 1982, 92 per cent of all electricity was coal generated, as compared with only about 20 per cent ten years earlier when power production was almost 30 per cent lower. It was partly the marked excess capacity in generating plant that made conversion on such a large scale possible. (Just as in the UK, actual demand for electricity lagged far behind the installed capacity, which had begun to be erected at a time when the continuation of high growth rates was expected.)

The plant conversions were undertaken without subsidies, on purely economic grounds, and the payback period of the conversion investment varied between two and four years (dependent on whether the plant was originally built for oil firing only or incorporated a system that, even though it originally burnt exclusively oil, admitted coal after certain alterations).

The advance of coal played a major role in the reduction of oil's share in primary energy, from over 90 per cent to 65 per cent in the ten years to 1983. A growing part of this oil supply is now coming from the Danish sector of the North Sea; recoverable reserves are not high and production is likely to peak in the second half of the 1980s, when it may cover 40-50 per cent of the expected demand for oil, the use of which will continue to decline under pressure of the planned further relatively modest advance of coal and of natural gas which will come on stream by 1985. The foreseeable quantity of offshore gas will exceed Danish requirements and will be exported to Sweden and Germany under already existing contracts. The initial impediment to the use of natural gas was the lack of a supply network since gas was not a popular fuel in Denmark, its use being restricted to relatively small pockets of town gas users. It was only in 1979 that the Danish parliament agreed upon the establishment of a natural gas supply network. The price of natural gas has been set at the heat equivalent price for gas oil but domestic consumers will receive a 10 per cent discount in order to encourage them to be connected.

Because of the country's industrial structure (the limited importance of heavy industry) and climate, space heating made up about 40 per cent of primary energy use in the mid-1970s. Nearly all of this was provided by oil boilers or oil-fired district heating (DH) units. Under the 1979 Heat Supply Act this situation has changed as consumers are connected to district heating, many of them utilising waste heat from power stations (combined heat and power, CHP) or to natural gas supplies. The actual situation in 1981 and the developments in the following twenty years, as 'prescribed' in the 1979 Act, compare as follows:

Table 4

Space heating in Denmark

	1981	2000		1981	2000
Space heating requirements, PJ	214	218	By system: per cent		
By fuel: per cent			DH heat only	25	20
oil	87	47	CHP/DH	15	35
coal	8	17	waste heat	5	5
gas	2	27			
renewables	3	9	total	45	60

Source: as for table 5.

The country's long historical experience of DH, developed largely on a cooperative basis, helps considerably in this planned expansion. The first DH system began operating some sixty years ago; there are now about 400 municipalities and communities with DH schemes installed, including CHP systems using waste heat from many of the country's power stations. The latter were backed by municipalities which supported DH (heat only) solutions as well, whilst the main heating cooperatives built DH plants for heat supply only. In relation to the population, the Danish DH network is probably the most extensive, particularly that of Copenhagen. One report [4] writes:

> Concern has been expressed in such countries as Britain, which have negligible district heating development, that lack of consumer acceptance might erode the economics of any proposed schemes. Something of the reverse has been a concern in Denmark. There, long established DH grids providing inexpensive heat have meant that CHP/DH is perceived by consumers as the inexpensive, reliable heat source, whilst natural gas is viewed as expensive and more problematical.

As it is envisaged, the natural gas grid will not compete with CHP/DH for customers in the same area. Power station waste heat through CHP/DH will go to the most densely populated areas; the less densely populated ones should receive natural gas, whilst elsewhere, in areas of sparse population, oil heating will remain to the extent that it can compete with electric heating and renewables. Since many consumers have no choice, the pricing of heat from the two sources, DH and gas, is an important issue and taxes of various magnitude have been levied on oil, electricity and also on coal for district heating; this obviously helps gas, although it has been presented as part of the conservation programme.

Pricing, taxation and financial incentives have been the main levers in the conservation effort. The incentives, mainly grants, run into very substantial amounts. Stringent thermal standards for new buildings have been introduced and efforts are being made to bring existing buildings up to these standards by the end of the century. This is being done in two ways. Firstly, a three-year declining grant programme has been introduced aimed at the rapid upgrading of residential properties; and secondly, from 1985 the seller of any property is obliged either to produce an 'energy certificate' issued by a (government-certified) energy consultant documenting that a required standard has been established, or to have the property inspected by such a consultant and inform the buyer of his findings.

All these efforts have continued without relaxation since the reduction of the oil price in March 1983. The results achieved by 1982 are worth noting:

Table   5

The Danish energy economy: selected indicators 1972-82

(1) Per cent changes in Danish energy consumption, 1972-1982		(2) Per cent shares in total use		
			1972	1982
Total primary energy use	-9	Oil total	93	62
Heating	-26	imported	92	52
Processing	-27	domestic	1	10
Transport	+1½	Coal	6	33
Electricity generation	+37	Other	1	2
Non-energy use	-36	Imported electricity	-	3
Oil use	-40	For comparison with other countries*		
Coal	+397		1973	1983
Other	+125	Oil	91	66
		Coal	9	34

Source for Denmark: The Danish Economy and the energy problems, The Economic Council, June 1980; O.W. Dietrich and O. Smith-Hansen, Formulating Danish Energy Policy, paper delivered to the Workshop on Formulating energy policy, International Energy Agency, November 1983; C. Johnson, Denmark's energy policy, Coal and Energy Quarterly, no.38, Autumn 1983; Danish energy plan and various government documents.

* For the last two rows: BP Statistcal Review of World Energy, 1984.

FRANCE

Heavily dependent on energy imports, the French have made the boldest attempt in Europe to build up a vast nuclear generation capacity. Indeed, the special feature of energy management in France is to be found not so much on the demand side - where they have applied the usual incentives and regulators - but on the supply side; provisional results indicate the outcome of this policy.

Table   6

The French energy pattern

	Per cent shares in total supply 1973	1983
Oil	68	49
Natural gas	8	14
Coal	16	14
Hydro	6	8
Nuclear	2	15

Source: BP Statistical Review of World Energy, 1984.

Under the Giscard administration the French economy embarked on a very ambitious nuclear development plan, creating an industry which now covers the whole spectrum and employs over a quarter of a million people. France is now second only to the US in world nuclear capacity and generation. The original plan's target was to replace 73 million tonnes of oil by nuclear power in 1990; this was reduced by the Mitterrand government to 48 million tonnes oil equivalent, but even so it remains unique in Europe. The target seems feasible since plants already under construction will almost certainly be completed. But even the reduced target puts Electricité de France (EdF) into the oddly difficult position of having a large and growing excess capacity as the end of the decade approaches.

By 1990, total generation could reach 430 TWh; for consumption, there are various estimates centering on 330 TWh and even one that assumes faster economic growth than now appears likely goes no further than 370 TWh. Thus the excess capacity is very large indeed. Nevertheless, the building of further power stations will continue at a slower pace in order to keep the nuclear industry going.

This large excess capacity originates not so much because national output is lagging behind earlier expectations, although this has been a contributory factor (French GDP rose by 25 per cent from 1973 to 1983), but rather because of the more efficient use of energy: demand fell by about 3 per cent in the same period. The cyclical recession/stagnation affected heavy energy using industries more than others, resulting in reduced energy use, but even taking this factor into account the results of the conservation effort appear very respectable. This is due to the combined effect of the fairly comprehensive legislative and regulatory programme for conservation and the successful operation of the strong specialist institution, the 'Agence pour la Maîtrise de l'Energie'.

There is likely to be an oversupply of natural gas also, due to successful conservation. Indigenous gas resources are being slowly exhausted and in order to cover growing demand the French have contracted for large imports from Algeria and the USSR. It seems that the quantity of gas contracted from these sources will exceed domestic requirements by about 1987-88.

The future excess availability of both electricity and gas is surely partly due to the lower-than-expected output and better-than-foreseen conservation. However, critics say that whilst the French government has invested/contracted heavily on the supply side, there has been little investment in converting equipment to use these fuels on the demand side, particularly by the private sector.

In view of this situation plans for further expansion of hydro capacity (mainly on the Rhône) have been suspended. Similarly, the earlier objective of maintaining 30 million tonnes domestic coalmining capacity has been dropped.

Output of the very heavily subsidised Charbonnages de France (CdF) fell from about 30 million tonnes in 1973 to around 20 million tonnes in recent years. An additional quantity of 24 million tonnes of imported coal was consumed in 1982. Of the total of 46 million tonnes, 16 million was used by EdF, 12 million by the iron and steel industry, 4 million by other industries and 14 million by other users. By the end of the decade, coal consumption will be lower and the needs of Edf will be halved since present usage includes that of thermal stations temporarily reconverted to coal, to be replaced by nuclear generation. (It is interesting that EdF found it worth replacing oil by coal in stations that would be taken out of mainstream operations within a few years.) The iron and steel industry will also need less coal because of technological changes, non-industrial use is bound to fall quite markedly and although industrial coal demand will probably go up (in the cement industry and a few others, as well as in new district heating systems) the increase should not be more than 3-4 million tonnes at most, very far from balancing falling demand in the other sectors. Both CdF production and imports will fall as a consequence. CdF will have the additional problem of utilising their low quality coal, a large part of their output, which so far can only be used in EdF power stations.

The French 'renewables' programme is also the most ambitious in Europe. It aims at a contribution amounting to 13 million tonnes oil equivalent by 1990. The main means to achieving this lies with the development of biomass and solar energy, with smaller additions from wind and geothermal sources. Solar heating is stimulated by considerable incentives. Another project is that of 'carburol' an alcohol substitute for oil-based motor spirit to be produced as methanol from agricultural materials, such as maize, straw, wood and waste, as well as special crops grown on poor quality land. In order to reduce petrol consumption, it is also planned to produce methanol from refinery coke, a residual of the processing of heavy crude oils, or even from imported coal. It is difficult to assess the likely outcome of all this, but some success seems probable.

THE NETHERLANDS

Although the Netherlands has for some time been one of the very few European energy exporters, thanks to the huge Groningen gas field, ever since the first oil shock (when oil deliveries to the Netherlands were boycotted by Arab suppliers) the Dutch have made consistent efforts to reduce energy use in general and oil consumption in particular.

Table 7

The energy pattern of the Netherlands

Per cent shares in total supply

	1973	1983
Oil	54	43
Natural gas	42	48
Coal	4	8
Nuclear	-*	1

Source: As for table 6.
* Less than ½%.

Apart from the generally known measures to reduce the use of energy, there are some points which deserve mention. Particular attention is being paid to the 'de-industrialisation' aspect (how to counteract the 'Dutch disease' that hits industry in the first place); the government considers the Dutch export pattern relatively energy intensive [5] and 'within the framework of the selective growth policy, the necessary and anticipated structural change of industry should be guided in a less energy-intensive direction, inter alia by means of the price policy, innovation policy and by promoting energy efficiency, among other things, by means of an energy supplement under the Investment Account Act. This energy supplement is 10 per cent above the basic allowance on investment, applied to certain energy conservation systems. Energy audits are encouraged: the government refunds two thirds of the audit cost if the results are made public.

The official policy recognised at an early stage that the interest of the individual firm can diverge from the 'national interest', as it indeed does, in view of the different price development. 'The aim is to carry energy conservation further than the point of individual cost-benefit equilibrium, namely as far as the social cost-benefit ratio remains acceptable.'[5] Where necessary, special financial government support is given to bridge the difference.

In the same 1979 government document, targets for energy saving were fixed for three benchmark years, 1985, 1990 and 2000, for the various types of consumption (domestic, and so on). One important means to achieving this in the area of household consumption is through district heating, mainly by utilising waste heat from electricity generation. (According to Dutch calculations, the average saving in fuel required to generate electricity and heat separately is 20-25 per cent, whilst compared with space heating alone the saving may be as high as 55 per cent.) The target for 1990 is to connect 350,000 homes to district heating and by 1979 projects involving 110,000 homes had been given the go-ahead.

Despite the earlier full closure of Dutch coalmines, coal also plays some part in the plans, in order to diversify supplies, but it will be imported.

The main preoccupation of the Dutch government in recent years has been the depletion of the large gas fields. After having started to export their gas on a large scale (providing more than 40 per cent of all domestic supplies) there were years when the Dutch, whilst honouring their export contracts, followed a more cautious marketing policy with a view to prolonging the life of their gas, and even developed gas imports. More recently, however, they seem to have been backing down on this policy, probably as a result of the easier world energy situation and the discovery of offshore gas. These latter supplies, although costlier than onshore gas, are being developed for preferential use with the unchanged intention of conserving onshore reserves.

Apart from gas, oil has also been discovered and started flowing towards the end of 1982. Although relatively small, the oilfields in the Dutch section of the North Sea may cover, after full development, some 15-20 per cent of requirements.

It is worth mentioning that the Netherlands' success in attaining some oil production, despite the original lack of geological promise, stems from having a tax regime which is favourable to explorers in the sense of allowing all but the very smallest finds (of gas, as well as oil) to be considered commercial; oilfields with reserves as small as 30 million barrels can be developed to send their product through costly pipelines.

SWEDEN

In the early 1970s, two thirds of Sweden's energy requirements were imported and the remaining one third was covered by hydroelectricity, the combined contribution of coal and nuclear power being about 3 per cent. By 1983, oil's share had been markedly reduced, the quantity of coal more than doubled, hydropower production was lower (partly due to unfavourable hydrology), but nuclear generation had increased to almost one fifth (though this may potentially be a problem because of the decision to move away from nuclear power after 1990).

Table 8

Shares in total Swedish primary energy supplies

	Per cent shares in total supply	
	1973	1983
Oil	64	51
Coal	2	4
Hydropower	33	27
Nuclear	1	18

Source: As for table 6.

In the same period total energy consumption was reduced by 15 per cent, while national output (GDP) rose by almost one sixth.

Part of this relative energy saving was the result of the declining production of the iron and steel industry, one of the country's most important energy consumers; from its peak in the mid-1970s, until 1982, steel output fell by one third.   This alone, however, would not explain the considerable energy saving and even less the reduction of oil use. These were the result of a combination of pricing and other policy measures undertaken within the framework of the country's energy policy.   (According to some reports, after the initial success of non-price policies, their effectiveness may have been waning recently.)

Grants, loans and tax incentives support the conservation programme in industry and elsewhere.   A special state board is responsible for information and training; the same board handles grants for demonstration and prototypes, the promotion of energy-efficient technologies and of the replacement of oil by solid fuels.   There has been a separate oil-substitution fund since early 1981, financed through a special fee on oil use, providing favourable loans and also grants. (Since the bulk of electricity is generated by hydro and nuclear plant, conversion of thermal stations to coal is far less important in Sweden than in many other countries.)

Conservation in the transport sector is supported by speed limits, progressive taxation according to the weight of the car, energy labelling of all new cars and measures to aid public transportation.

A ten-year programme aims at reducing residential energy use by 25-30 per cent by 1988; grants and loans are available to house owners, who can receive free advice from well-trained building inspectors and other municipal staff, for improved insulation and the instalment of more efficient heating systems; new building regulations have been introduced and the importance of district heating has been stressed. The latter now covers about one quarter of all heating requirements and, although much of it is still based on oil, conversion to coal, peat and some other sources (wood, heat pumps) is under way.

Energy policy on both the demand and supply side is backed by a comprehensive research programme. Although many aspects of the consuming side are well covered by this programme, its more noteworthy parts concern the supply side. It is hoped that fuel switching could replace 9 million tonnes of oil by 1990: a further 3 million tonnes of oil might be replaced by peat and wood waste, 3 million tonnes by coal imports, 1 million tonnes by solar energy, 1 million tonnes by increased use of electricity and 1 million tonnes by new district heating schemes, mainly for Stockholm. In the longer run a quadrupling of energy derived from forests is expected; plans include special plantations of fast-growing trees, with regional processing centres to

32

turn them into chips as fuel for power plants and appropriately constructed industrial boilers.

JAPAN

Of all the countries studied, perhaps the most spectacular results have been achieved by Japan, where indigenous energy production in the early 1970s accounted for no more than about 9 per cent of demand. From 1973 to 1983, Japanese national output rose by over 40 per cent, whilst energy use declined marginally. The energy pattern also changed markedly.

Table 9

The energy pattern of Japan

	Per cent shares in total supply 1973	Per cent shares in total supply 1983
Oil	77	60
Natural gas	2	7
Coal	15	19
Hydro	5	6
Nuclear	1	8

Source: As for table 6.

The serious impact of the rise in the oil import bill is clearly reflected by the use of energy in Japan: before the first oil crisis energy demand rose by 11 per cent a year, afterwards it slowed to 3 per cent a year and in the three years after the second oil price shock it showed a significant decline.

One factor which is often mentioned by students of the 'secret' of Japanese economic success, which helps to explain their results in the

33

energy area, is the nature of Japanese society itself, which is probably unique among advanced industrial countries. It is characterised by strong national consciousness, social cohesion, and cultural homogeneity which combine to make Japan a consensual society. Energy efficiency has become a national goal, supported by everybody under the guidance of the government.

As one report has put it, [6] 'In spite of her position in the per capita league table, Japan's past poverty is still reflected in her poor housing stock and her citizens' thrifty habits. They are still inclined to deal with winter cold by wearing more clothes and to accept that summer is a time for sweating'. 'Japan is a country where the author of an official report, wanting to say "the whole nation should make efforts to ..." can easily slip into the traditional phrase: "the officials and the people together should make efforts to ..." without anyone thinking the phrase the least odd.' In other words, the situation in Japan is not quite the same as anywhere else; if an objective is sponsored by the government and generally accepted, it will be pursued with conviction and enthusiasm. This has characterised the approach to the energy problem too.

From the outset the Japanese government has looked energetically for ways of reducing consumption in general, and of oil in particular. In fact a law dating from 1951 has already encouraged the efficient use of energy and required factories to employ trained qualified technicians for heat control. This was repeated in 1979 in a considerably updated and revised form, specifying the required qualifications and the responsibilities of the energy managers. (More details on this scheme will follow in the next section, page 44.) Certain standards were set for industrial plants; MITI officials have the right to check company records concerning the internal energy economy and, if dissatisfied, can 'instruct' the firm to mend its ways. There were standards set for insulation too; target efficiency standards were set for cars, refrigerators and air conditioners, to be reached at various points in time (for example, car makers by April 1985, car importers by April 1988).

Tax incentives and credit provisions support the governmental measures, being applied in a discriminatory manner in favour of energy-saving investment. (Since tax depreciation allowances in Japan are, in general, much less generous than in the UK, there is more scope to discriminate in the desired direction.)

To an extent, the business cycle has helped to achieve energy saving on a national level, in particular affecting the most energy-hungry industries such as steel, aluminium and heavy chemicals. But there is also a definite endeavour to change the economic structure in favour of more energy-efficient activities, at the cost of the heavy users. It is doubtful whether the Japanese steel industry will ever return to its former peak production; aluminium production dropped by 70 per cent from 1979 to 1982 and it is believed that most of the smelters that were closed down will never be reopened; the production of ethylene fell by about one third in the same period, again with a question mark over its return to the previous higher level. In other industries too a long term approach has been encouraged and supported in order to introduce new technology and the transformation of the production process so as to reduce, among other things, energy use.

In 1982, Japan accounted for almost three quarters of the world's total imports of liquid natural gas (LNG). Gas usage, often including liquid petroleum gas (LPG) is further promoted, as is the use of coal -mainly imported - and the expansion of nuclear capacity. In 1982, construction started on 10,000 MW of new generating plant, half of it thermal, 40 per cent nuclear and the rest hydro; two of the thermal plants will burn coal and one LPG. The build-up of geothermal power is on the agenda and nuclear capacity, probably reaching 26,000 MW by 1985, should increase - with the approval of the Japanese Atomic Energy Commission - to 46,000 MW by 1990 and 90,000 MW by the year 2000. Even if these targets are not quite attained they reflect the 'nuclearisation' effort (interestingly, at a time when the opposite attitude can be observed in the United States).

Similar large-scale development is envisaged to expand port capacity for coal imports, since the capacity of coal-fired power stations is expected to rise from about 6,000 MW in 1981 to 26,000 MW by 1990. The cement industry has already been converted almost wholly (90 per cent) to coal, the pulp and paper industry is expected to follow, and shifts from oil to coal are also foreseen in other industries.[7]

These plans are supported by a wide ranging research and development programme, extending from the better utilisation of coal to the search for the best engineering solutions to utilise renewables.

BELGIUM

Originally, the Belgian energy base consisted solely of coalmining. However, coal production has for a long time been in decline (and the remaining industry is probably the most highly subsidised in Europe). The relative success of the energy management - energy saving in general and the reduction of oil use by one third, in relation to national output - has been due to the forceful conservation campaign supported by attractive financial incentives for both industrial and other consumers, to nuclear energy that provides about one quarter of electricity, and to the programme for converting oil-fired power plants to coal. The decline of the importance of the iron and steel industry has been another contributory factor.

Table   10

The Belgian energy pattern [a]

| | Per cent shares in total supply | |
	1973	1983
Oil	62	48
Natural gas	16	19
Coal	22	21
Nuclear	-	12

Source: As for table 6.

[a] Includes Luxembourg.

IRELAND

Prior to 1981 Irish energy consumption was moving ahead of GDP: by 1983, however, energy use related to national output had been reduced by one fifth. Apart from some conservation measures, the change was presumably at least partly due to the coming on stream, since late 1980, of offshore natural gas from the Celtic Sea, an efficient and easily controllable fuel. This has greatly changed the energy pattern.

Table 11

The energy pattern of the Republic of Ireland

	Per cent shares in total supply 1973	1983
Oil	73	50
Natural gas	-	22
Coal [a]	24	26
Hydro	3	2

Source: As for table 6.

[a] Commercial solid fuels only (bituminous coal, anthracite and brown coal/lignite).

Ireland is Europe's biggest producer of peat, which is not included in the above figures. If peat is converted on a calorific basis to oil equivalent, the share of all solid fuels in the above table would rise to over a third.

NORWAY

In relation to the size of the Norwegian economy, oil and gas production is very substantial, making this country's energy economy unique among the developed countries. The huge energy 'saving' is partly due to the upsurge of the oil and gas output in the Norwegian sector of the North Sea (this inflates GDP with less than proportional addition to energy use) but conservation efforts should not be underestimated. Given the abundance of oil and gas, the conservation programme and its result have been remarkable, as well as the endeavour to reduce the use of oil and the further development of the country's traditional energy source, hydropower.

Table 12

The Norwegian energy pattern

	Per cent shares in total supply	
	1973	1983
Oil	31	23
Natural gas	2	2
Hydro	67	75

Source: As for table 6.

The UK Compared With Other Energy Exporters

In the previous sections of this paper the energy use of many countries has been related to national output, including the UK indicators. It is of particular interest, in concluding this analysis, to compare the pattern of primary energy use in the UK with that of other energy exporting countries within the OECD. There are not many: Germany (still a coal exporter although a major net importer of fuel), the Netherlands and Norway in Europe, Canada and Australia outside Europe.

In many respects, the German pattern of energy use is the most similar to the British. Both countries are major producers of coal (actually, the only ones in Western Europe), both rely increasingly heavily on natural gas, have raised their nuclear capacity, and both lack noteworthy hydroelectric resources. The changes in the energy use in the past ten years are also very similar, as indicated in table 13.

The Dutch economy relies now even further on natural gas than earlier, but has stepped up the use of coal and started nuclear generation in order to reduce the use of oil.

The similarity with Norway ends with the development of production in the respective sectors of the North Sea, since otherwise Norway covers the bulk of domestic energy requirements by hydropower. Despite the abundance of indigenous oil, the Norwegians, like the British, have been aiming at reducing oil usage.

The Canadian and Australian economies are in many respects different from those of the European energy exporters, yet the two main features characterising the energy economies of all the countries included in the table are the reduced use of oil and the relative saving of energy (in the latter case with the exception of Australasia). The switch away from oil has been very similar: oil's share in each country was reduced by around one quarter in the first ten years after 1973, and the relative energy saving in the four European countries was also comparable with the reduction by about one fifth in the UK.

Table 13

The energy pattern of selected 'energy exporters' in OCED

	Germany 1973	Germany 1983	Netherlands 1973	Netherlands 1983	Norway 1973	Norway 1983	Canada 1973	Canada 1983	Australia[d] 1973	Australia[d] 1983	UK 1973	UK 1983
Oil [a]	57	44	54	43	31	23	44	32	52	38	49	37
Natural gas [a]	10	16	42	48	-	-	22	22	6	15	12	22
Coal [a]	31	32	4	8	2	2	8	14	34	37	35	34
Hydro [a]	1	2	-	-	67	75	24	26	8	10	1	1
Nuclear [a]	1	6	-	1	-	-	2	6	-	-	3	6
Total [b]	265	250	77	68	28	34	191	209	67	88	225	193
Energy/GDP [c]	100	80	100	77	100	78	100	89	100	108	100	79

Source: as for chart 1.

[a] Per cent share in total primary energy supplies.
[b] Million tonnes of oil equivalent.
[c] Index, 1973 = 100.
[d] Includes New Zealand etc. ('Australasia').

Selected Aspects of Energy Policy

It would be a crude oversimplification to attribute any country's results in reducing energy use related to output to any one factor, such as, for example, 'nuclearisation' in France. The energy economy of the countries covered is much more complex and the 'results' and 'achievements' have been the outcome of a whole host of measures taken by governments and energy suppliers, as well as of the reaction of consumers; the possibilities stemming from their different situations and endowments also varied widely. Under the pressure of high energy prices and the (rational or irrational) expectation of the insecurity of supply there have been changes in every single country, some as a reaction to governmental measures and others as the rational outcome of consumers' behaviour. The intentions 'from above' have generally, but to a varying degree, met with readiness 'from below', albeit often hesitantly, to result in relative energy savings. Beyond this generalisation, however, the two streams of factors influencing energy use have differed by country in both kind and degree.

The United Kingdom fits quite well into the overall picture and her place in the 'league' of energy savers is respectable, as the comparisons in the preceding charts and tables indicate. Many of the measures taken in other countries, though not all, have been applied here too, although often in a different form or to a different degree. Nevertheless, the study of the energy policies of a fairly large number of countries yields certain points worth mentioning which have either not (or not yet) received comparable attention in the UK or could point to new departures which may seem worth considering. To list them, in a few cases in some detail, is the purpose of this section.

FINANCIAL INCENTIVES

The strongest incentive for increasing the efficiency of energy use is the high price of energy (high, that is, as compared with the situation prior to 1973, both in energy terms and as related to the general price level). As already mentioned above, the pricing policies in the various countries have not been covered in this study; this section is restricted to other financial incentives.

In practically every country there is some form of fiscal incentive to new investment, usually through tax relief. Less frequently it is a straight grant. Investment in energy appliances or equipment aimed at energy saving generally enjoys some sort of preferential treatment with regard to taxation, even though the degree of this differential taxation varies by country. (In some countries, however, no distinction is made and the tax relief on energy projects is no different from any allowance given to investment in general.) There are, however, specific arrangements in a number of countries for energy investments, such as

- special incentives for heat recovery, CHP and 'biomass' in Austria;
- grants of up to 40 per cent of the costs of investment in conservation, the switch away from oil and the use of waste heat in

Denmark;

- support given to the installation of solar panels, as well as heat pumps, grants to small scale hydro-electric plants and the purchase of electric cars in Italy;

- credits and 'regulatory incentives' to help the introduction of energy production from 'renewables' in the United States;

- in the Netherlands, two thirds of the costs of the energy audit are refunded if the results are made public;

- in New Zealand there is a graduated sales tax on cars based on engine capacity and a punitive (30 per cent) sales tax on air conditioners;

- in Australia all non-oil heating appliances, as well as ethanol-fuel, are exempt from any tax.

TESTING/CHECKING OF EQUIPMENT

The conservation effort in many countries is supported by mandatory regulations that prescribe the <u>testing</u> and <u>checking</u> of energy-using equipment. Such a regulation can take different forms. Some are relatively simple, such as

- combustion tests on boilers exceeding 50 kW capacity (Ireland);

- temperature control in work premises (Luxembourg);

- obligatory energy audit for users consuming more than 1000 tonnes of oil or equivalent (Portugal);

- or compulsory efficiency standards for oil burners (Switzerland).

Elsewhere, however, the situation is more complicated: in Denmark, for example,

- all oil-fired heating appliances below 120 kW capacity must be cleaned, tested for efficiency and adjusted if necessary once a year

45

(obligatory requirements of a slightly different nature exist for oil appliances of higher capacity);

- public entities were required to prepare plans by the end of 1982 for bringing their buildings up to an 'acceptable state of thermal efficiency' by 1987;

- buyers of apartments and houses after 1 January, 1985 must be presented with either a certificate showing that the dwelling meets current heating efficiency standards or the report of an energy consultant stipulating the work required to bring the building up to standard. [8]

ENERGY MANAGERS

The definition of an 'energy consultant' is blurred; that of the 'energy manager' is clearer in quite a few countries, including the UK. But whereas here the energy manager is usually appointed by the management of the (industrial or other) company or organisation, the Japanese follow a different practice which deserves attention.[9]   In Japan, every single 'listed' plant is required to have a qualified energy manager; a plant is listed for this purpose if it consumes more than 3,000 kilolitres of oil or equivalent, or 12 million kWh of electricity.   In 1980 there were 2,300 plants listed for oil and about the same number for electricity, accounting for about 70 per cent of total industrial energy usage.   The qualification required to become an energy manager is granted by MITI, which prescribes the curriculum and organises the examination by a panel of experts.   Prerequisites are at least one year of relevant work experience and a training course organised by the Energy Conservation Centre.[10]   Such a course may take eight days (or two days a week for four weeks) and is followed by ten hours of written examination over two days. (There are shorter -six day - courses ending with a one day examination for those with at least three years' relevant work experience or for graduates in a relevant subject.)

The Japanese energy manager has considerable standing within his company (the management is required to 'give due respect to his opinion') and is also obliged to keep very detailed records of all aspects of the plant's energy economy, including, among other things, the energy consumption rating of every single piece of equipment. The company's failure to have an energy manager or to keep these records properly could incur considerable fines. MITI officials are authorised by law to have access to all these records; if they find that the plant's energy consumption is markedly substandard they may require the firm to prepare an energy rationalisation plan and have their own means of gently forcing the plan's implementation. All this, however is fundamentally based on the notion that the energy manager is <u>qualified</u> to do his job properly, an arrangement that has presumably contributed significantly to the Japanese achievement in the area of energy saving, especially in industry

In a different area, Swedish building inspectors and other municipal staff are trained in three-week courses, with periodic follow-up to give home-owners free advice regarding the most cost-effective conservation measures.

TRANSPORTATION

After industry, the transport sector is the largest user of energy, consumed chiefly by the ubiquitous motor car. Though it is generally accepted that public transportation of persons, and in many cases also of goods, is more energy-efficient (depending on the load factor) than fragmented private transport, there are not many countries where the energy programme includes direct reference to specific support of urban or rural public transport. (A few exceptions can be found however: New Zealand is one of them, as is Norway where more than one third of the total cost of the public transport network is covered by state subsidies.) In a number of cases major new investment has been made on an underground network, not so much to save energy as to solve mass transportation problems into and within larger cities. However, in at least as many cases existing public transport systems requiring huge subsidies are being partially liquidated in view of the severe and successful competition from private transport.

Taxation plays a major part in the endeavour to limit fuel consumption of automobiles; both the fuel and the vehicle are usually heavily taxed, the latter often according to engine size or weight. In many countries also there are either mandatory requirements or voluntary undertakings by the carmakers aimed at raising engine fuel efficiency (see below).

Some measures follow orthodox lines, directly or indirectly limiting the use and performance of cars, such as speed limits, limited business hours at petrol stations (Brazil), varying taxation on cars discouraging the use of large engines, and so on. Car 'pools' are encouraged in some countries (Finland, New Zealand) and the search for alternative, that is non-oil based, sources of energy has already yielded some modest initial success. Possibilities for oil substitution are technologically rather restricted and projections for the year 2000 still show almost 100 per cent oil dependence by the road transport sector of most countries. Research and development have been active in this area (and should be promoted), nevertheless, some attempts are worth mentioning.

The best known alternatives are the electric car and the use of various forms of alcohol/methanol as motor spirit. The electric car is not a new idea; the problem is to extend its range and speed and to solve the inconvenience of refuelling.

Among the countries pursuing this line, Italy deserves a mention. Here a 20 per cent grant is given to public bodies for the purchase of electric cars. The Brazilian 'gasohol' programme is well known and also the most successful among the many ventures aimed at 'replacement' fuel; a significant part of the car fleet has been running for some time on 'gasohol' produced from sugarcane that is either mixed to conventional motor spirit or is used direct in converted engines.

The same idea is being followed in other countries less well endowed with base material (no other agricultural produce is so well suited to alcohol production as sugarcane). Elsewhere, the conversion of cars to the use of CNG (Canada) or LPG and even straight natural gas (New Zealand) is the aim of the research and development work.[11]

In the United States there are mandatory requirements for improving the fuel economy of new automobiles; the 1985 target is 27½ miles per US gallon (= 8.6 litres per 100 km) of gasoline, certainly an improvement on the 1982 standard of 24 mpg. But, as the IEA states, even with that new target the average efficiency of new US cars would remain below other large IEA member countries, particularly Japan

49

(8.1 litres per 100 km).[12] In Germany the car industry has pledged to increase the fuel efficiency of new cars by 10-12 per cent, and possibly 15 per cent, by 1985, compared with the 1978 level, in addition to continuing its search for alternative motor fuels.

CONVERSION TO SOLID FUELS

The main area within which conversion is taking place is in industry, particularly in power generation, which is the largest user of oil. Denmark has largely replaced oil by coal in power stations and the retrofitting investment calculations showed a payback period of only two to four years. India has introduced a total ban on oil or gas use for power production. Other energy hungry industries have also been in the forefront of the conversion effort: the Swiss cement industry, for example, has switched entirely to coal, and the building material industries in other countries are also well on the way to substantially reducing oil usage, in general by turning to coal.

The processing of coal into gaseous and/or liquid fuel, an area where the Germans were pioneers (with no generally diffused success) many decades ago, has again become important. Whilst, for reasons of its own, the old type of coal conversion into liquid fuel has been in full force only in South Africa, the search for better, more efficient methods has received considerable stimulus from the changed energy situation. It is not surprising that Germany has been pushing hard in the area of R & D aimed at coal liquefaction, though the achievement of British Gas in coal gasification at their Westfield, Scotland station probably puts BGC at the head of this technology.

The increase in coal transportation has posed new problems and requirements; in some countries the rail system has had to be upgraded for coal transportation, for example, in Canada (in a westerly direction);

- work has been advancing on coal slurry pipelines;
- coal exporters, such as the US and Australia, have had to invest in new or enlarged port facilities;
- some of the importers may be facing similar problems at the receiving end: the establishment of a common import centre for Scandinavia (possibly in Norway) is being seriously considered, where large carriers could unload coal for distribution to final consumers.

In a few countries the exploitation of domestic resources has been (or is planned to be) stepped up in order to reduce reliance on imported coal, directly or indirectly; this is the aim of the peat programmes of Ireland and Finland which include not only additional production but also the development of better methods of utilisation as well (for example, briquetting, improved stoves, and so on).

Consumers are, naturally, restricted in their attempts to switch away from oil since existing appliances generally determine the kind of fuel they have to use. In this area it is worth mentioning - as just one result of the present wide-ranging research effort - that only recently the launching of a new type of boiler has been reported[13] enabling coal to be burned as efficiently as oil or gas and, at the touch of a switch, to be able to change from burning any one of these three main fuels to another. One of the most pressing problems for increased coal use concerns its effect on the environment, since the cost of the large-scale introduction of environmentally acceptable technologies is high - whether they are established and proven methods (such as flue gas disposal) or new processes (for example, fluidised bed combustion).

51

STOCKHOLDING

The stockholding of oil has been regulated by the recommendation of the International Energy Agency, and accepted by its members. Under this agreement governments of the countries involved undertook to keep stocks of oil covering 90 days of their national net import requirements. For the UK this means zero. However, the EC have a stocking obligation of 90 days of consumption (as distinct from imports) with an adjustment for indigenous production; under this provision the UK obligation is 76½ days of consumption. Some countries have gone further along this road. In Finland, for example, larger users are obliged to hold certain quantities of coal, apart from oil products.

Finally, two particular aspects require special attention: the often twinned aspects of combined heat and power (CHP) and district heating (DH), and the efforts to tap energy from 'renewables'.

COMBINED HEAT AND POWER/DISTRICT HEATING

The idea of CHP is simple. Even the most modern power station operates with no more than 35 per cent 'thermal efficiency'. This means that only 35 per cent of the theoretically available heat in the fuel import is converted into useful electric power. Of the remaining heat, some 10 per cent goes up the chimney and 55 per cent passes into the condenser cooling water. This is the case in the best designed and most efficiently operated stations. From a technological point of view, if a low grade fuel, such as coal, is converted into a high grade form of energy, such as electricity, some of the energy content of the fuel is rejected in the process as low grade heat. It is, of course, sensible to use this rejected heat, if possible, since otherwise the heat is 'wasted'; CHP is one means of utilising it.

There are several calculations comparing the performance of separate heat and power production with CHP. A British and a German source can be quoted in simplified form:

Table 14

Comparison of performance

(i) UK [a]	Fuel used	Electricity generated	Usable heat	Heat rejected
Separate heat and power:				
ordinary power station	100	35	-	65
boiler plant	100	-	80	20
total	200	35	80	85
Combined heat and power	200	56	104	40
Advantage of CHP	-	+21	+24	-45

(ii) Germany [b]	Fuel input	Power available	Heat available	Total input utilised
Condensing turboset	100	32	-	32
Backpressure turboset in CHP	100	17	68	85
Advantage of CHP	-	-25	+68	+43

Source: [a] Third report of House of Commons Energy Committee, 1983.
        [b] S. Schindler, 'Rational use of energy and oil substitution with particular
             emphasis on electric energy in the Federal Republic of Germany', in
             International Co-operation for rational use of energy in industry, The Lima
             Seminar, July 1983, IEA/OECD.

Thus CHP makes possible a 'thermal efficiency' much higher than generally achieved at the best thermal power stations.

The idea of DH is even simpler: it is the central heating of not one house but a group of houses (or other premises) or a whole district. This wider-ranging 'central heating' can be supplied from a purpose built plant or the heat can be taken over from other plant, usually a power station, which produces (but cannot itself use) heat in great quantities. Hence the frequent marriage of CHP and DH.

Both CHP and DH play important roles in the plans and practices of many other countries. Some examples follow:

- in Austria, wherever possible, generation is tied to CHP and DH schemes; where it is possible for consumers to connect DH, no tax incentive is provided for other changes; in Vienna, off-peak electricity is estimated to be 26 per cent, gas 75 per cent and heating oil 104 per cent more expensive than heat provided by DH (but it is admitted that DH involves large initial investment);
- in Denmark, one of the pioneers of CHP, where the first scheme started operation in the 1920s and where to date six major cities and some 400 towns have community heating, the objective is to supply half of the whole country's heating needs by DH in the not too distant future;
- in Finland, about 80 per cent of dwellings in the capital, Helsinki, are connected to DH networks; some 30 per cent of the nation's heating requirements are supplied by CHP/DH and it is intended to raise this to 50 per cent within about fifteen years;
- in Germany, 1.4 million dwellings are connected to DH networks (about

8 per cent of national space and water heating, including DH supplied public and commercial buildings); coal fired co-generation (CHP) plants are in the programme which also aims at some kind of integration of electric power, gas and DH supplies from CHP;

- in the Netherlands, an ambitious programme of CHP is in operation and DH is being promoted in various ways - 17 DH schemes, some of them linked to CHP plants have recently received subsidies; the price of DH is linked to the price of heating by natural gas so that customers will never pay more for DH than they would using natural gas for heating;

- in Hungary, a very large part of the dwellings in the capital, Budapest, is connected to DH and the heat is supplied partly from power stations, partly from hot springs.

Some data about the Finnish schemes should serve to indicate CHP's versatility in terms of capacity, fuel use and the consumers served:

Table 15

Selected indicators of CHP/DH patterns in Finland, 1981

	Percentage of totals
(i) Capacity	
Heat only output capacity in connection with electricity generation	31
Direct heat output of power station boilers	14
Heat output capacity of stationary heating plants	39
Heat output capacity of transportable heating plants	16
Total DH capacity	100
of which: connected load of consumers	78
(ii) Fuel use in DH	
Coal	36
Fuel oil	44
Natural gas	4
Peat	12
Wood	2
Other (including urban refuse, residual from woodpulping, other industrial waste heat)	2
Total	100
(iii) Heat production and consumption	
Production direct from boiler	45
Production by turbines	55
Production total	100
of which: distribution losses	9
consumption of DH	91

***

	Percentage of totals
Consumption by dwelling houses	60
industrial buildings	10
other consumers	30
Total	100

Source: Finnish Heating Plants' Association, Helsinki.

In contrast to these (and other) countries, the advantages offered by CHP or DH are hardly being exploited in the UK. Neither of these systems has, for some reason, become popular.

A small number of CHP and DH schemes have been in operation for some time, such as the Pimlico DH system, supplied from Battersea power station since 1950; Spondon power station near Derby has been providing heat to the adjoining Courtaulds factory since 1960; commercial fish farms have received heat from Hinkley Point and Drax stations since 1977-78, and the latter also provides heat to a large greenhouse/tomato plant complex nearby. There are a number of other smaller systems but, in the aggregate, CHP or DH account for a very small part of heating requirements. Even in the case of entirely new major developments, such as the Barbican in the City of London or the new town of Milton Keynes, the initial investigation into the possibilities of CHP was discarded.

The potential of CHP and DH, as a means of saving energy on a national level has been recommended several times by various investigators. The Marshall report[14] recommended the drawing up of a CHP/DH strategy; the Atkins report repeated this recommendation and suggested that the system should be introduced in 'lead cities';[15] the House of Commons Select Committee on Energy believed that CHP 'is the best of options when economics, comfort, fuel efficiency and long-term environmental benefits are taken into account';[16] individual MPs have also taken up the subject, saying, among other things, that whilst 'millions of people cannot afford enough energy to heat themselves to a decent standard ... yet, within sight of their homes, we have a system of producing electricity whereby two thirds of the fuel put into power stations is thrown away by surplus heat ... that is enough to heat every building in Britain';[17] and, for particular cities, a special report suggested simpler solutions.[18]

Yet so far nothing much has happened. One of the often heard criticisms cites investment costs being particularly high in Britain where the majority of people live in family houses, whose connection to a DH network would require more capital than in the case of continental cities where multi-storey apartment blocks accommodate the majority of the population. This may be so, although in some of the countries mentioned above where DH is widely operating the system of 'family houses' like those in Britain is certainly not unknown and the existing or planned schemes - extending to embrace a large part of the Danish or Finnish heating requirements - include areas of a population density similar to that in Britain.

Prices may also provide a partial explanation of why CHP/DH has been, and is, backward in the UK; fuel was cheap (first coal, then oil and later natural gas) and there was no incentive to promote other than individual heating systems in the past, the latter believed to be easier to control independently. However, this reference to prices has now become invalid. There may also be institutional reasons: the statutory duty of the electricity supply industry has always been to produce electricity, if possible, cheaply. Hence there has been a trend towards the centralisation of electricity production in scattered, giant power stations, many of them away from the populated areas which are the market for heat.

It appears, therefore, that CHP and DH represent a largely untapped potential for better energy economy in the UK, although requiring major

investment.   So far advance has been very slow.   By about the middle of
1984, altogether 74 CHP schemes have been submitted to the electricity
supply industry which acts as a consultant on new CHP schemes (and the
Electricity Council has recently set up a separate CHP bureau).   Of
these 74 schemes not more than 4 have been implemented, 26 wholly
abandoned and 44 are being 'reconsidered' or have been postponed or
shelved.   The   reasons   for   non-implementation   have   been   chiefly
economic, indicating that if progress in this area is desirable more
attractive incentives, or perhaps some other financing structure, may
be required.

RENEWABLES

In an impressionistic (and unavoidably) somewhat arbitrary manner,
table 16 indicates those sources of renewable energy that the countries
surveyed seem to pursue.   Their opportunities for exploiting renewable
energy sources are clearly limited to a large extent by geography and
natural endowment, even though these limits may be less strict and
prohibitive than generally believed.

It is, for example, obvious that countries in a sunny climate are
better placed to capture solar energy than those further north; yet,
many countries not enjoying subtropical or tropical sunshine devote
attention and allocate resources to its exploitation - such as, for
example, the Scandinavian and Alpine countries.   With the possible
exception of heat pumps (for which the indications in the table are
presumably incomplete), the tapping of energy from wind and biomass
appear to be the most popular methods.   Hydro, geothermal and tidal
energy are largely determined by the endowment of particular countries
with these resources and, to an extent, plans based on wood, including

60

re- or afforestation, are in the same class.   Apart from the better known Brazilian practice, a handful of other countries is also experimenting with replacing gasoline as motor spirit by alcohol or methanol.

Some of the countries have fairly concrete targets - or at least guidelines which are more than wishful thinking - for the harnessing of various kinds of renewable energy.   Some of these are as follows:

- Denmark expects that five per cent of energy requirements will be covered by renewable sources by 1995, whilst

- Belgium hopes to reach this by the year 2000;

- Austria reckons that solar energy and heat pumps will contribute five per cent to supplies in the early 1990s;

- France plans to obtain the equivalent of 13 million tonnes of oil equivalent from renewables (including the production of their 2.5 MW experimental solar power station) by 1990; and

- in Canada renewables (excluding hydro) are targeted to provide six per cent of total energy use by 1990.

Table 16
Renewables [a]

	Solar	Heat Pumps	Wood [b]	Wind	Hydro [c]	Tidal	Geo-thermal	Alcohol, methanol	Biomass, biogas	Waste
Austria	+	+		+	+*				+	
Belgium	+			+					+	
Denmark	+			+			+		+	
Finland [d] [e]	+	+	+	+	+*					+
France	+			+					+	+
Germany	+	+		+			+		+	
Greece	+			+						
Ireland [d]						+				
Italy	+	+		+	+*		+		+	+
Netherlands	+			+						
Norway	+			+					+	
Portugal	+									
Spain	+									
Sweden [d]	+		+					+	+	
Switzerland	+	+	+							
Canada [d]	+		+		+					+
Japan	+			+	+*		+	+	+	
New Zealand	+			+			+	+		
US	+						+			
Yugoslavia	+									
Brazil [f]	+		+	+	+			+	+	
Egypt	+		+	+	+				+	
India	+			+	+*		+		+	
Indonesia					+					

62

Table 16 (continued)
Renewables [a]

	Solar	Heat Pumps	Wood [b]	Wind	Hydro [c]	Tidal	Geo-thermal	Alcohol, methanol	Biomass, biogas	Waste
Kenya	+									
Sri Lanka	+			+	+					+
Thailand	+		+	+	+*					+
ECOWAS [g]	+		+		+					

Source: National energy plans, as appended.

[a] The table is incomplete in the sense that it lists only those renewables that were given a significant mention in the countries' plans or programmes. Heat pumps, for example, are being followed up as a possibility in many countries but only the documents of the few countries indicated above mention them with any (arbitrarily assessed) significance in their plans. Exceptionally, a few unusual non renewables have also been included in the footnotes.

[b] Includes reforestation, the introduction of fast growing trees and the use of wood as charcoal. There is some unavoidable duplication between 'wood' and 'biomass'.

[c] Those marked with an asterisk (*) mainly mean 'small hydro schemes'.

[d] Also peat promotion programme (Finland, Ireland, Sweden and Canada).

[e] Graphite shale (Finland).

[f] Oil shale (Brazil).

[g] The Economic Community of (sixteen) West African States, listed on page 118.

There are certainly some points worthy of mention in the area of renewables as they figure in the countries' plans or programmes. Nevertheless, it cannot be denied that this whole sphere is still in need of the solution to many problems of technology and engineering before commercial viability on a scale big enough to make a marked contribution to supplies is attained; in almost all cases the exploitation of renewable energy is somewhere in the Research-Development-Design pipeline - more advanced in some countries than in others. In this sense, some of the possible departures are no further than the development of newer technologies for nuclear power generation, more efficient and safer than those in operation today.

Some of the plans may never materialise, such as the Irish endeavours to harness the tidal energy of the Shannon, which would require investment on a very large scale (possibly sharing the fate of the Severn tidal scheme in the UK). Some of the other hydro schemes appear more promising, especially the 'small' ones envisaged in Italy, Japan and elsewhere. Japanese reports qualify their solar and geothermal solutions as 'almost ready for practical use'. Solar energy has great potential in the sunny countries, such as Egypt, Kenya, and so on, but their use there, though spreading, is still very limited. The instruments for promoting solar energy are also varied: in New Zealand, for example, a five year interest free loan is being offered for the installation of solar water heaters.

To some extent it is understandable that a country such as the UK which is well provided for a time with domestic energy sources of the conventional kind should lag behind others in the search for the exploitation of renewable energy. It may seem prudent to let others do the groundwork whilst we are in the happy position of being able to 'wait and see'. But whilst it is arguable that this may be, for the moment, the right attitude to take, it is also undeniable that the UK is not in the forefront of the search for an energy solution to the possible approach of the 'post oil' era.

The grants allocated from central funds to research and development of renewable energy have so far been relatively small, as shown in table 17. The table also demonstrates how the early hopes attached to extracting energy from the sea have gradually been, rightly or wrongly, scaled down and the allocated resources re-channelled from waves to wind and geothermal energy.

Table 17

Allocation to R&D of renewable energies in the UK

	1978/9	1979/80	1980/1	1981/2	1982/3	1983/4
Total, £m	2.6	6.8	9.1	15.0	12.2	11.9
distribution per cent						
wind	12	9	9	6	20	40
waves	69	44	36	29	25	8
aquifers	4	19	15	17	12	-
hot dry rocks	4	-	10	38	25	36
solar	8	18	10)	7	12	10
biofuels	-	1	3)		5	6
tide	3	9	16	2	-	-
hydro	-	-	1	1	1	-

Source: Department of Energy and Financial Times, 21 December 1983.

Despite the relatively modest resources allocated, some initial results have undoubtedly been achieved, such as the small experimental wind turbine in Carmarthen Bay (with a rated output of 0.2 MW), the advance of the geothermal projects in the South of England, or the increasing number of solar panels on buildings (understandably also mainly in the South of England). These, however, are no more than meek, if praiseworthy, beginnings; major projects, such as harnessing tidal power in the Severn Estuary, have not yet passed the point of a conclusive feasibility study, again for possibly good reasons, such as the enormous investment requirement running into billions of pounds, and the environmental impact. There are admitted risks in such a major venture, which would take more than ten years to bring to fruition (as indeed would other renewable schemes before they could make a marked impact on energy supplies).

Thus, it is not surprising that the possible contribution of renewables to UK energy supplies is much smaller than those taken into account, on a more or less realistic basis, in other countries' plans. It is not easy to pinpoint expectations, but it seems that they do not exceed half to one million tonnes of oil equivalent by the end of the century.[19]

As for the more remote future, it is clearly difficult to assess what the UK's 'renewable possibilities' are. ETSU's futurologist estimates (or guesses) for the first part of the next century are more optimistic but of course their basic condition is that by then the technological and engineering problems will have been overcome and decisions will have been made in due course for financing the various developments, bearing in mind the long gestation period of any major energy scheme.[20]

Concluding Remarks

By a happy geological accident the UK is in the rare position of having conventional energy resources for some (historically short) time, even after the peaking in the mid 1980s of oil production from the presently operating or developed North Sea fields. While we are therefore quite well placed to 'sit back' and let others make the running in the search for new energy resources, there are two points to remember: first, any major new energy project takes a very long time to materialise; and second, in the meantime it is worth considering measures that could yield a more immediate result by conserving energy and thereby prolonging the present favoured state of relative abundance - a situation that many other advanced countries would obviously welcome.

It is, therefore, prudent to survey the approach of these other countries towards their own energy problems, at present more pressing but in the long term basically comparable to those the UK will have to face in due course. This is the purpose of this paper. In many respects the measures taken elsewhere are similar, at least in kind if not always in degree, to those in the UK, although there are a few departures that have not yet been explored here. Some of them may warrant deeper study and consideration, whilst others may seem to deserve rethinking in the light of other countries' practices and experiences.

Appendix: National Energy Programmes

OECD-EUROPE	OTHER OECD	DEVELOPING COUNTRIES
Austria	Australia	Brazil
Belgium	Canada	Colombia
Denmark	Japan	Egypt
		India
Finland	New Zealand	
France	United States	Indonesia
Germany		Kenya
		Korea (South)
Greece	CENTRALLY PLANNED	Sri Lanka
Ireland		
Italy	Hungary	Thailand
	Yugoslavia	West Africa
Luxembourg		
Netherlands		
Norway		
Portugal		
Spain		
Sweden		
Switzerland		

Note: The intention of these abstracts of the national energy programmes was not to repeat them in their entirety but to select those aspects that appeared worth noting. These are usually listed under two main headings: supply and demand/conservation, the latter including financial incentives aimed at energy saving or oil substitution. In some cases there is an unavoidable overlap between the two main categories.

AUSTRIA

Supply

Apart from hydro-electricity, supplying about one quarter of energy needs, domestic resources are small and about 60 per cent of requirements are imported. (The only nuclear station, with 692 MW capacity, has been mothballed since the 1978 referendum; it may take two years to put it into operation.)

The USSR is the present source of gas supplies.

The search for oil, gas and coal has strengthened, further hydro-projects (mainly small), solar and wind energy have also been supported, as well as heat pumps. There are also taxation incentives for heat recovery, CHP, biomass, etc.

The official expectation is that solar and heat pumps could provide five per cent of energy needs for heating in the early 1990s.

Demand/conservation

Fuel switching (to coal, DH and gas) and conservation are the main elements of policy, supported by various measures.

Pricing is a heavily used instrument (with the exception of coal, all fuels are subject to control). Car tax depends on engine size. Electricity in the eastern part can be 60 per cent more expensive than in the hydro based western provinces.

Conversion of power stations to coal or coal/gas is being actively pursued. Generation is tied to DH and CHP plans. Where there is a possibility for consumers to connect to DH, no tax incentive is provided for other changes. Calculations show that in Vienna DH is cheap: off peak electricity is 26 per cent more expensive, gas 75 per cent, heating oil 104 per cent - but it involves large initial investment.

Both new thermal stations built as replacements for the nuclear plant are subject to environmentalist protests.

There are tax incentives for conversion of oil fired appliances and energy saving equipment.

Five day consultancy service freely offered to industry.

District Heating Promotion Law (1983) offers public funds to promote new investment in DH and CHP.

'Fuel efficient driving' included as an item in driving test.

Legislation makes tenants in rented accommodation financially interested in energy saving.

Compulsory energy labelling of major household appliances. Air conditioning requires official authorisation.

BELGIUM

Supply

The only domestic resource is coal, but Belgian coal production has declined steadily. Although domestic production still provides 40 per cent of total domestic demand, this production is maintained by high government subsidies.

The nuclear programme is being expanded and is forecast to provide 60 per cent of total electricity requirements by 1986, the highest percentage of any IEA country. There is a continuing programme for the conversion of oil fired generation to coal.

Renewable energy is hoped to contribute under five per cent to energy supplies in the year 2000. Encouragement is given to projects involving solar and wind energy.

Demand/conservation

Most energy prices to Belgian consumers are regulated.

Oil use is expected to decline in industry through to 1985 and electricity is expected to increase. Oil use has also declined in the transport sector, the factors responsible being the reduction in average car size and an increase in diesel cars.

There appears to be potential for increased use of CHP but its competition with gas seems to be a major constraint.

Companies may claim 35 per cent of the cost of most conversion/conservation investment as a tax reduction.

Progressive vehicle tax by engine size.

DENMARK

Supply

Oil imports predominate in an economy with a very high, but declining, reliance on imports. Final energy demand is greatest in the residential/commercial sector, mainly for heating. Oil and gas deposits have been found in the Danish North Sea; these should enable Denmark to reduce import dependence from nearly 100 per cent to 70 per cent by the end of the decade. The oil pipe line from the Gorm Field will be fully operative by 1985. Natural gas from the North Sea and heat from power plants will become the most important elements of heat supply over the coming decades.

Coal has largely replaced oil as a fuel for electricity generation and further expansion is planned. Denmark's harbours are being enlarged in order to receive coal ships up to 175,000 dwt. Industry is not, however, suitable for large scale conversion to coal as it consists mostly of small, dispersed enterprises.

The future of nuclear energy has not yet been decided. If introduced, its effect would be to slow the rate at which new coal powered generation was needed.

Demand/conservation

Intensive conservation efforts applied since the mid 1970s are beginning to show results. A combination of energy pricing and the provisions of the Industrial Energy Bill have been responsible for these results. Under the latter, grants can be given up to 40 per cent of the costs of investment in conservation, switching away from oil and the use of waste heat.

During 1981-2 there have been the following changes:

- All oil fired heating appliances below 120 kW must be cleaned, tested for efficiency and ajdusted if necessary once a year (obligatory requirements also exist for oil appliances greater than 120 kW).

- Public entities are required to prepare plans before the end of 1982 for bringing their buildings up to an 'acceptable state of thermal efficiency' by 1987.

- To be eligible for the maximum energy saving subsidy, the report of a certified energy consultant is no longer required. This homeowners' subsidy is exempt of income tax.

- Buyers of apartments and houses after 1 January 1985 must be presented with either a certificate showing that the dwelling meets current standards or the report of an energy consultant stipulating the work required to bring the building up to standard.

District heating is fairly well developed and is intended to supply more than half of all heating needs. Work has started to convert three quarters of a million residential oil burners to other fuel. The government's hope is that, in future, the heating for the sparsely populated areas in residential and public premises will be provided either by natural gas or by surplus heat from power plants. Investment grants for purchases of renewable energy equipment have been increased from 20 to 30 per cent. The Danish 'renewable' energy programme has concentrated mainly on wind, geothermal, solar and biomass energy sources; these may provide almost five per cent of TPE by 1995.

The new hydrocarbon tax results in taxable income varying from 40 per cent of net income in marginal fields to 83.5 per cent in highly profitable fields.

Since 1973 the oil requirements/GDP ratio has been reduced by almost 50 per cent. The next decade should see a further diversification of energy sources and a continued drive for energy efficiency. For this, public transport has been (is planned to be) made more efficient, mainline electrification is planned, the relative prices of coal and fuel oil have been changed and all new base-load power plants will be coal fired.

FINLAND

Supply

Under the earlier plan, from 1978 to 1981, the share of oil and coal was reduced, nuclear and hydro raised significantly, peat and other sources (wood, etc.) marginally. Domestic contribution (including nuclear) rose from 30 to 46 per cent.

New plan in 1983. Regulated stockholding of oil and also of other fuels. Coal transport facilities have been - and will continue to be

73

- improved and coal use may double by the early 1990s. Hydro power expansion planned on a limited scale. Advanced refining of domestic fuels is aimed at, for example, compressed peat; technology of production and use of peat and wood developed, including standby equipment for using peat, the large increase of which is planned through a state-owned peat producing and marketing company and encouragement of private small scale production. Farming of fast-growing species of trees to be stepped up, the procurement system reorganised and the competitiveness of wood based fuels maintained (including the possibility of wood based power plants).

Other domestic sources will be pursued: wood based waste slurries from the forest industries, heat pumps, solar (!), wind and graphite shale.

Natural (Soviet) gas is unpopular because of its high price; imports lagged behind the agreed limit. Extension of the pipeline to the Helsinki area and further to the West is possible and would add to gas use, but there is no decision on this as yet.

Further collaboration with other Nordic countries - aimed at a joint electricity utilisation system - is planned. Coal will probably play a larger part in supplying the rising need for electric power. Legislation on obligatory stockholding of importers and large users will be implemented concerning crude oil, oil products and coal.

About 100 MW of new base-load capacity will be needed in the early 1990s. Nuclear generation more than doubled from 1980 to 1983 and its further expansion is one possibility; another is coal.

Demand/conservation

Finland is one of the world leaders in DH: some 30 per cent of all homes (and 80 per cent in Helsinki) are linked to DH. This may rise to 50 per cent nationwide by the year 2000. One basis for this expectation is the further considerable expansion of CHP, another is the building of heat supplying plants or conversion of existing power plants.

Motivation to intensify conservation is to be reinforced (in view of the decrease in the real price of energy). Testing of the performance of energy saving devices will be introduced for consumer protection. Car pools are legally encouraged.

Domestic fuels are not taxed; imported energy, on the other hand, is subject to tax. It is intended to take into account the environmental impact of each type of fuel.

Low interest loans are offered for oil replacement in industry and district heating; these have started to move from oil to coal and domestic fuels.

FRANCE

Supply

France imports over two thirds of total energy requirements. Indigenous resources are meagre: oil reserves are modest, reserves of gas are small and the coalmining potential limited and declining. The country is in a stronger position with regard to reserves of uranium and hydro electricity.

France is the only country to have embarked on a full programme of 'nuclearisation' under the Giscard administration; the Mitterrand government did not essentially modify it in principle. (The programme consisted not only of the building of a whole host of nuclear reactors for generation but extended to the whole range of activities that precede and follow the actual building of the plants - indeed the most sophisticated nuclear set-up in Europe.) Modification was made necessary, however, not because of a change of policy but because of demand lagging behind expectations. Plans had to be downgraded but no concrete new and accepted plan has so far been made public.

The 1990 capacity of Electricité de France is already determined by the existing plants and those in the course of construction (though some of the latter might be delayed); it clearly shows the shift towards nuclear.

Generation capacity	1981		1990		1990 Index 1981 = 100
	GW	%	GW	%	
Hydro	19.6	28	26.1	23	133
Nuclear [a]	21.6	30	59.1	52	274
Other thermal	29.7	42	27.8	25	94
TOTAL	70.9	100	113.0	100	159

[a]   Including a 200 MW prototype fast breeder.
      Source: Synthèses des premières conclusions du Groupe long terme énergie établi en Avril 1983, Sécrétariat Général du Plan, dated 5.5.1983.

According to this, EdF will have considerable excess capacity by 1990.

The utilisation of solar power is being actively pursued. France's 2.5 MW Themis solar energy power station near Targasonne was finished in 1983. The cost of producing electricity from this installation is extremely high and the government is financing research into more cost efficient solar power projects.

According to plans, by 1990 the contribution of renewable energy should be between 5.4 and 9.8 mtoe; apart from solar, this includes biomass (wood and vegetable matter), geothermal, and 'waste' heat utilised in new district heating systems. This was later raised to altogether about 13 mtoe, including the output of the solar power station.

Demand/conservation

Attention has been given to energy conservation. An energy independence plan was approved by the French parliament in October 1981. One of its aims is to reduce the share of petroleum in total consumption from half to less than a third by 1990. A powerful conservation policy has been pursued mainly through the 'Agence pour la Maîtrise de l'Energie' which is perhaps the strongest conservation institution in any OECD country. Its work is supported by a comprehensive legislative and regulatory programme for conservation.

The energy demand projected for 1990 in 1981 is unlikely to be realised much before the year 2000. The change is shown in the table below and obviously means fewer new nuclear stations. Even so, both coal and oil based generation will be reduced. Hydropower may be further expanded.

Primary energy demand, mtoe	1983 consumption	1981 plan for 1990[a]	New scenarios for 1990[b] low	high
Coal	24.3	35.5 (31.5)	23.0 (17.0)	28.0 (23.5)
Oil	89.3	77.1 (66.2)	62.0 (58.5)	66.0 (62.5)
Gas	24.8	29.2 (27.3)	28.3 (23.5)	29.3 (25.0)
Nuclear	27.4	59.8 (57.5)	55.2 (54.0)	59.7 (56.5)
Hydro, etc.	15.2	(17.4) *	(17.0) *	(21.0) *
TOTAL	181.0	219.0(206.0)	185.5(180.5)	204.0(196.5)

Note: The figures are central values of the ranges given in the various sources. The figures in brackets indicate the lower end of the

forecast range. Hydro etc. is treated there as a residual.
[a] The Hugon Report.   [b] Source: Les Echos, 23 March 1983.
                     * Not given in source.

GERMANY

Supply

Net oil imports dropped considerably to 1981, but this drop is slowing down. Substitution of coal for oil has now slowed after the completion of conversions in the building materials industry, where the substitution to date has been most successful.

Gas consumption has increased, with indigenous production contributing one third of total requirements. The main suppliers of gas are the Netherlands, the USSR and Norway. In September 1982 a long term contract was signed with the Norwegian company Statoil for annual gas imports of 15 billion m^3 to be delivered from 1986. Lignite accounts for 30 per cent of German coal production and is mainly used in electricity generation. Domestic hard coal production is not competitive with imported supplies. Preparations have started for the planning and construction of a demonstration plant for coal liquefaction.

No disposal facilities, at present, are a constraint to nuclear expansion. Those being built will be important assets, as will progress on the integrated waste management scheme. Nuclear capacity of 26 GW by 1990 is projected.

Contracts between the domestic coal mining industry and the electricity utilities stipulate fixed purchase commitments; this is supported by subsidies and a levy on electricity consumption paid by consumers (4½ per cent of price).

Demand/conservation

All relevant craft-curricula have been adapted to energy conservation.

Grants given for energy auditing and up to 75 per cent of consultancy cost, solar heating, heat recovery, for new technologies as well as for coal-firing in electricity generation and the improvement of energy efficiency in residential/commercial buildings.

World recession in the early 1980s has hit at industrial activity in Germany and as a result reduced TPE requirements. Conservation measures, such as increased thermal insulation standards for new buildings, have also been contributing factors.

Energy prices are not regulated in general. Two major exceptions are subsidies on domestic coal prices and electricity tariffs to small scale consumers.

TPE requirements in 1981 were slightly lower than the 1973 level, in spite of an increase in real GDP of 17 per cent over the 1973-81 period. Conservation efforts in the space heating market of the residential sector have played a significant part in this decline.

In the transport sector, higher fuel efficiency and shorter travel distances have reduced energy consumption. The car industry's voluntary commitment was to reduce fuel use in new cars by 15 per cent from 1979 to 1985. Energy saving driving is included in the test curriculum. Car pools are encouraged. Speed limits: 130 km on motorways, 50 km in cities.

DH accounts for eight per cent of the energy required for space heating and water heating. Besides public and commercial buildings,

1.4 million dwellings are connected to DH networks. The government has adopted a programme for the extension of coal fired co-generation plants with sizeable financial incentives. It is also aiming at the integration of electric power, gas and DH supplies from CHP.

GREECE

Supply

The government's energy policy places great emphasis on the reduction of oil imports and the maximum utilisation of indigenous resources.

The production of solid fuels is to increase, lignite in particular. Recoverable lignite and peat reserves are in excess of 500 mtoe. The substitution of coal for oil in industry has resulted in a surplus of heavy fuel oil.

Hydropower plants represent 29 per cent of total electrical capacity. Nuclear power is not yet on the agenda. Imports of natural gas are not foreseen in the energy balances of the present five year plan.

Exploration activity continues, the latest discoveries of oil and gas being made at Katakolo. There are four refineries operating in Greece, one of which is state owned. Their total capacity is more than double the yearly demand for oil products.

Wind and solar power are being considered as alternative energy forms. Pilot units already operate at Kythnos and Crete. Importance is also being placed on improvements in infrastructure (coal ports).

Recent measures for the protection of the environment include:
- Reduction of the sulphur content in heavy fuel oil to 0.7 per cent.
- Reduction in the lead content of gasoline to 0.15 g/litre.
- Substitution of heavy fuel oil in industry with town gas.

Such measures represent a heavy burden on the national budget.

Demand/conservation

Grants or other incentives are offered for solar installations, certain investment projects aimed at conservation, retrofitting in residential etc. buildings in the colder zones.

CHP in power stations is being studied.

By 1992, all oil-firing in power stations should be eliminated (except on isolated islands) by lignite based and hydro stations.

IRELAND

Supply

Ireland is heavily dependent on imported oil, which accounted for 58 per cent of TPE in 1981. This dependence may be reduced in future years with the present oil discoveries off the coast at Waterford. Until now, the most significant indigenous energy sources were natural gas from Kinsale Head field and peat.

Irish coal reserves are low quality and small. The increasing use of coal is dependent upon imports.

Hydro-electric power contributes only three per cent of TPE. The bulk of the new base-load electricity generation will be coal fired. No decision has been made on the construction of a nuclear plant.

Wind machines for the electrification of isolated communities and tidal power extraction in the Shannon estuary are two possibilities for alternative energy supplies.

Demand/conservation

Energy pricing policy is important to the Irish government's programme on energy conservation. All town gas companies are subject to full price control. The government has revised the pricing system of peat produced by Board Na Mona (State Peat Board) in order to enable it to finance the development of peat extraction. Oil products are subject to excise duty and VAT: other fuels are free of tax.

In 1981 the industrial sector consumed about 25 per cent of TPE and 26 per cent of total primary oil requirements. To reduce energy consumption in this sector, a second series of combustion tests on industrial and commercial boilers over 50 kW is being conducted.

Prototype testing of a multi solid fuel closed stove to be used in dwellings is now under way.

To improve energy efficiency in the public sector there has been a modernisation of the bus fleet in the Dublin area where the suburban rail network has been electrified.

There is financial support to fuel efficiency surveys, demonstration projects in industry, CHP installations, public transport, and for the encouragement of solid fuel in residential/commercial buildings.

The speed limit is strict: 88 km/hr generally.

ITALY

Supply

With scant indigenous energy resources, Italy is heavily dependent on oil imports. Imported energy satisfies 82 per cent of primary energy demand.

The country's only significant domestic energy resources are hydro electricity, geothermal energy and natural gas. Government price controls operate over many forms of energy.

Increasing use is being made of coal, nuclear energy and natural gas. The gas industry is aiming at a 65 per cent increase in supply by 1990, four fifths of which would be provided by imports. Plans are being made to increase the nuclear power capacity to 6 GW. AGIP Carbone has been responsible for the improvement of coal infrastructure, but major coal imports are still needed.

If agreement is reached, the USSR could be supplying a third of natural gas imports by 1990. At the time of writing the Italians are so swamped with imported gas that they are now channelling it into power generation.

Activities in the field of renewables include:
- Operation of the first prototype solar power plant in Sicily;
- the support of a wind energy project, its purpose being to supply energy and drinking water to the small islands.

Biomass is still at the experimental stage.

Oil has recently been discovered fifteen miles off the coast of Southern Sicily. The find, operated by Montedison, is substantial relative to Italy's current oil production of under 40,000 b/d and its estimated reserves of 625 million barrels.

Demand/conservation

Incentives for fuel switching measures are provided in the Law of Energy Conservation (1982). Fuel switching measures include installation of solar panels and heat pumps, and grants for small scale hydro electric power plants. Other provisions of the Law include:

- grants of up to 20 per cent for municipal bodies for the purchase of electric cars;

- the labelling of household and heating appliances;

- interest bonuses on capital grants aimed at saving at least 15 per cent of hydrocarbon or electricity use;

- capital grants up to 50 per cent of demonstration projects using renewable sources or energy saving prototypes in industry and agriculture;

- funds for CHP or 'renewable' feasibility studies and up to 30 per cent grants for the actual project and the same grant for energy saving air conditioning and the use of renewables in existing buildings; 10 per cent reduction on the 1980 situation of fuel use in new cars; progressive licence fees in relation to size, 50 to 110 km/hr speed limits.

Upgrading of (mainly urban and inter urban) public transport systems, particularly railways.

LUXEMBOURG

Supply

Apart from a limited amount of hydro electricity, Luxembourg has practically no indigenous energy sources. The major industry, steel, consumes over 50 per cent of TFC. The world steel recession and the switch from oil to alternative fuels have reduced energy requirements.

The majority of coal imports is from EC countries. To reduce dependence on a limited number of suppliers, holdings have been purchased in overseas coal mines.

Natural gas supplies are assured for the coming years. The distribution system, confined to the city of Luxembourg and the southern part of the country, limits the extension of gas use in the residential sector.

Electricity requirements in excess of the generation of hydro stations and steelworks are presently being supplied by Germany and Belgium. Contracts signed with these two countries expire in 1985 and Luxembourg must therefore reach an early decision on future electricity supply. One possibility is the sharing of one or more thermal power plants abroad.

Demand/conservation

Temperatures on work premises are now controlled. Compulsory monitoring of heating installations in public buildings with twice yearly inspection.

Financial assistance for pilot installations of heat pumps and other alternative sources including solar.

THE NETHERLANDS

Supply

In 1980, oil and gas accounted for about 45 per cent and 47 per cent respectively of TPE requirements, with coal and nuclear contributing 6 per cent and 1.4 per cent.

The Netherlands became a North Sea oil producer late in 1982. Union Oils Q/1 development is significant because it is the first of four projects which together could produce as much as 100,000 b/d. Efforts are also being made to enhance production of onshore crude oil through secondary and even tertiary techniques.

Oil production is encouraged by favourable taxes, these helping to make economic oilfields with reserves as small as thirty million barrels.

Further development is possible in the Netherlands' North Sea gas province and work is continuing on tying-in new deposits to the two main transport systems. There may be a reversal in the policy pursued by the Netherlands for the last decade of cutting back on exports while developing imports, in order to conserve indigenous gas.

The Coal Memorandum (1980) aims at reintroducing coal into the Dutch energy system, the R&D programme aiming to promote the commercial use of coal through fluidized bed combustion, co-generation processes, coal gasification, etc. Coal gasification is a strategic issue for the Netherlands since gasification would permit the use of an already extensive gas infrastructure for deliveries. The memorandum restates the 1974 proposal to build additional nuclear power stations. In 1985 the government and Parliament will consider the report of an independent steering committee and decide whether to proceed with the nuclear option.

Small scale wind energy systems have reached the stage at which commercialisation possibilities are being examined. A pre-feasibility study was recently submitted to the government on a large wind energy project combined with a hydro storage system. Solar energy and energy from waste are two other energy sources being developed. These schemes are expected to make a contribution to the reduction of energy imports after 1990.

Demand/conservation

The government intends to price natural gas at a premium over relevant oil product prices to reflect its advantages.

To encourage energy saving investments a 10 per cent 'energy bonus', in addition to the ordinary investment tax refund, became available for energy saving projects. For solar and wind projects this can now amount to 25 per cent, for coal projects to 15 per cent. Other financial incentives:

- subsidies up to 25 per cent of the investment cost of energy saving in the non-profit sector;

- 40 per cent grant of audit cost to smaller (less than 200 employees) companies;

- 50 per cent of feasibility study cost and 25 per cent 'risk sharing loan' for energy saving or substitution projects in industry;

- 67 per cent subsidy for industry branch audits if results are published;

- subsidies for higher efficiency central heating.

The Dutch operate an ambitious programme of combined heat and power (CHP) generation. District heating (DH) is encouraged and is promoted by government loans and subsidies. The price of heating by DH is linked to the price of heating by natural gas so that customers using DH will never pay more than if they were using natural gas for heating purposes. Some 20 DH schemes, some of them linked to CHP plants and others using waste heat, have received subsidies. To stimulate CHP in industry, continued deliveries of gas will be made available in coming years, with a temporary discount on the normal price.

During 1980, about 346,000 existing residences received financial aid for insulation. The original target was 200,000 homes per year. The scheme continues.

Taxes on motor vehicles are based on weight.

Compulsory standards for new residential and office building include ground floor insulation and double glazing (for dwellings).

NORWAY

Supply

Norway is more than self sufficient in energy and is a net exporter. The main indigenous energy resources are hydro electricity generation, oil and gas.

The use of coal, fuel wood and peat has increased. Biomass, wind energy and solar heating and cooling are potential energy sources.

Demand/conservation

Despite the abundance of resources, the government's attention has turned to energy conservation, the introduction of DH and the expansion of coal use.

The development of DH has so far been discouraged by Norway's low population density and the hydro electric potential. The rising costs of electricity and petroleum have altered the position regarding DH and DH feasibility studies have been made for major cities.

Oil requirements per unit of GDP have declined steadily. Prices for oil products in Norway were freed from government control on 1 January 1982.

The establishment of a common import centre for Scandinavia, where large vessels could unload coal for distribution to final consumers, is being considered.

Financial incentives:

- support for demonstration plants for conservation by government and also grants/loans for investment in industry and buildings by the Oslo Electricity Company;

- the setting aside of tax free funds is permitted for waste heat utilisation;

- certain energy projects are free of the general investment tax (10 per cent);

- energy produced by recovery or back pressure plant is exempt from the industrial electricity fee;

- public transport is heavily subsidised (more than one third of the total cost of the public transport grid is covered by state subsidies).

Speed limit: 30 or 50 km/hr in built up areas and 80 km/hr outside.

The government objective is to reduce power system loss from the present 17 per cent to 14 per cent by 2000.

PORTUGAL

Supply

The shares of both imports and oil in total energy are over 70 per cent. Hydro electricity and a small amount of solid fuel are the only domestic sources, apart from uranium mining (but there is no nuclear plant).

Coal exploration is forced; transport facilities present a problem. The 60:40 hydro:thermal balance may change to 40:60 by mid 1990s, raising demand for coal; nuclear plant discussed but opposition is strong (partly because of earthquake danger). In 1982, some 1,940 MW hydro and 1,260 MW thermal plants were under construction (including a 720 MW hydro plant). There is further hydro potential but not sufficient to cover the likely needs of the 'newly industrialising' country.

Solar energy is encouraged.

Demand/conservation

Some special features:

Intention of gradually dismantling the subsidies on fuel oil and gas oil.

Introduction of obligatory energy audit and management at enterprises using over 1,000 toe/year.

CHP projects (14MW) approved may only use residues or by-products, renewable energy or waste heat; commercial fuels only when more efficiently used than at public steam power stations.

Up to 50 per cent grants are given to industrial energy investment projects.

The World Bank is financing an energy conservation and diversification scheme, consisting of a wide array of projects, with a budget of $30 million.

The sales tax on cars above 1400 cm^3 is between 50 and 100 per cent of the sales price. Annual car tax varies according to age, cylinder capacity and fuel, with special tax on private diesel cars. Maximum speed limit: 90 km/hr.

SPAIN

Supply

Coal is so far Spain's most important indigenous energy resource. Further expansion of coal production is constrained by small and heterogeneous deposits and the very scattered nature of the coal mining industry. 80 per cent of coal is used in electricity generation. The ports of Gijon, Algeciras and Tarragona are being enlarged to ease the importation of energy supplies. An important environmental problem is the high sulphur content of Spanish coal.

Spain is heavily dependent on oil imports. There has been a reduction in oil imports from the Middle East and an increase in imports from West Africa and elsewhere. Domestic crude oil production is very limited.

The nuclear programme has expanded rapidly and nuclear power is expected to satisfy 40 per cent of total electricity generation in 1990.

Hydropower represents a quarter of Spain's domestic energy production. Among other renewable sources of energy, solar power is the single most important area of development. A public company, INISOLAR, has been created to improve and speed up market penetration of solar energy systems.

Demand/conservation

Energy conservation programmes focus on the industrial sector, which consumes more than half of TFC in Spain. The phasing out of oil fired plants and policies to increase the supply of non oil energy sources is expected to help in reducing the oil share in Spain's energy requirements from 60 per cent to about 45 per cent by 1990.

Next to light fuel oil, the single most important group of products are LPGs, which are being used in about 80 per cent of all private households. There are no plans for public or private DH.

The transport sector consumes 42 per cent of all oil; oil use per car is falling and car fuel efficiency is increasing. Speed limits are in operation on all roads.

SWEDEN

Supply

Only minor oil finds have been made on the island of Gotland. The programme on oil substitution is contained in the 1981 Energy Bill. Replacement of 9 mtoe is to be achieved as follows: coal and other indigenous fuels - 6 mtoe altogether; methanol, solar, heat pumps - 1 mtoe; electricity for heating purposes - 1 mtoe; Stockholm district heating - 1 mtoe.

Sweden has proven peat reserves of 270 million tonnes but its utilisation is restricted by transport difficulties. Pelletising of peat is being investigated.

At present the role of natural gas in towns is marginal and the market for natural gas in Sweden is unlikely to exceed 10 per cent of energy needs by 1990. Gas, imported from either the Soviet Union or Denmark, will be increasingly used in the heating market.

Infrastructure may be a constraint on coal use. Two 1,000 MW coal fired power stations are being built and are due on stream in 1984.

In one major solar development a central solar heating plant will heat 500 houses in Uppsala by 1984. Work is being carried out on the use of alternative motor fuels. The energy contribution of forest residue is also being promoted.

Demand/conservation

Conservation policies aim at voluntary savings by energy consumers rather than mandatory regulations. Part of the Building Code requires that windows must be triple glazed in all new houses and the window to surface ratio should not exceed 15 per cent. The average car fuel efficiency should improve from 9.0 to 8.5 litres/100 km by 1985. Speed limits are in force and the energy labelling of new cars is compulsory. Helped by taxation, insulation, installation of thermostats and wood chip fired boilers in homes, an estimated 250,000 t a year of heating oil has been saved.

Direct electric heating will be prohibited by the Building Code except for cases where additional savings can be proven. There is a proposal to replace oil in the DH system for the Greater Stockholm area, but no decision has yet been taken on the method to be used. Financial support is offered for energy projects involving alternative energy resources such as wood chips and biomass. The ambitious target is to reduce the share of oil in TPE requirements from 51 per cent in 1983 to 40 per cent by 1990.

The share of DH in Sweden's TFC may grow to 12 per cent (at present 7 per cent) by the mid-1990s. The construction of coal fired hot water plants in three main cities is being advocated by the government. The objective of the DH programme is 1,000 MW capacity growth per year, with 10 per cent investment subsidy.

The administration has increased the value added tax on energy and increased electricity costs through an extra tariff on sales from hydro power stations.

Financial arrangements:

- loans up to 50 per cent for oil substitution;

- up to 50 per cent grants for demonstration plants;

- 25 per cent subsidy for peat firing boilers, 50 per cent for plants processing forest waste, 15 per cent for heat pumps, 50 per cent for waste heat utilisation, 15 per cent insulation grant for house owners;

- loans for improving the thermal efficiency of buildings;

- funds for advisory services in agri-horticulture; - support for small hydro power stations.

Building inspectors and other municipal staff are trained in 3-week courses (with periodic follow up) to give home owners free advice regarding the most cost effective conservation measures.

SWITZERLAND

Supply

Hydro power is the main indigenous energy source. Imported oil accounted for 48 per cent of TPE in 1981. Economic constraints limit coal development.

From four per cent of TPE in 1981, gas is expected to increase its share to nine per cent by the year 2000. All gas is imported and 30 per cent of the gas imports in 1990 are expected to come from the Soviet Union. A gas find has been made at Finsterwald to provide the country's first indigenous gas supply.

Electricity is playing an important role as a substitute for oil. By the turn of the century it is expected to supply 32 per cent of industrial energy consumption. In the residential sector the use of electric heat pumps is expected to increase from the present 6,000 to 60,000 - 120,000 by the year 2000. The use of electric heaters should increase fourfold in the same period. Thermal power plants and pumped storage hydro plants will be used increasingly to handle the demand at peak times.

Since January 1982 solid mineral fuels have been submitted to compulsory stock regulations in order to increase security of supply.

Nuclear power has increased in importance over the last few years. However, nuclear power plants may have their licences for operation reviewed in 1985. New plants will not be given a licence unless the permanent and safe disposal of the radioactive waste can be guaranteed.

The transport sector accounts for 26 per cent of TFC and oil consumption in this sector is expected to double to 8.1 mtoe by 2000. Limitations on speed is one of the measures being investigated by the government to improve energy efficiency.

Demand/conservation
The federal government does not provide subsidies for energy conservation but almost all cantons provide tax allowances for energy saving and switching. Industries receive advice on energy from industrial associations and these organised training courses for the first time in 1982.

Customs duties are the strongest form of taxation on energy. The duties are high on gasoline and diesel oil, a turnover tax being levied on both. The government intends extending this to the fuels which have been exempt.

To encourage energy conservation, the government has published a model bill for cantons wishing to legislate for their own energy saving programmes. 55 per cent of the Swiss population now (1984) lives in cantons implementing compulsory insulation codes for new buildings, and 80 per cent in cantons implementing compulsory efficiency standards for oil burners. The National Energy Audit Programme provides house owners with information on conservation measures.

The cement industry has switched completely to coal. Coal use has increased and now accounts for 9 per cent of industrial energy. Further improvement may be possible if the supply of heat and electricity by coal-based CHP installations is considered.

District heating provides only a small share of total heat supplies (1.8 per cent in 1981) and the greater part of DH is supplied by CHP plants. Two major new DH projects are ready for construction (1984). The government is studying the possibility of setting up several wood-fuelled district heating schemes. These include a project to provide hot water for over 500 buildings.

The government is encouraging an education programme on the use of solar energy and also supports an independent solar information centre. Berne has introduced an energy law which allows the spending of Sw. Fr. 5 million per year to subsidise the use of new and renewable energies.

AUSTRALIA

Supply

Australia has generous indigenous energy resources of coal, natural gas and uranium and is able to supply almost two thirds of its own oil needs. Energy requirements are only three quarters of Australian

96

energy production, but oil imports continue to be necessary to meet current demand for liquid fuels.

Coal (both bituminous and steam coal) is Australia's most abundant energy resource. Progress has been made to meet skilled labour requirements, identified as a possible constraint to expanded coal production. The infrastructure necessary for coal transportation is being improved and there is an ongoing programme to develop or upgrade coal export facilities. State-owned railroads dominate coal movements.

Current oil reserves, including condensate and LPG, amount to 452 mtoe (331 mtoe commercially declared and 121 mtoe of non-commercially declared reserves). Good prospects exist for additional discoveries.

Natural gas is continuing to be substituted for petroleum fuels. Over three quarters of all natural gas consumption occurs in the industrial and electric utility sectors. The feasibility of linking the Bass Strait and Cooper Basin gas fields is being considered.

Australia has significant resources of oil shale. Gas liquefaction is another possible source of synthetic fuels.

Although the country has excellent uranium resources, there are no nuclear power plants in operation or planned. The current 26 GW of electrical generating capacity in Australia will be expected to handle the expected demand growth for electricity with the minor addition of new baseload coal-fired plants.

The government of Western Australia recently announced its decision to connect the Kalgoorlie gold fields with coal based generating facilities south of Perth. The hope is that this will replace 50,000 tonnes of petroleum fuels per year.

Demand/conservation

Two rather powerful programmes launched: the National Energy Conservation Programme and the National Industrial Energy Management Scheme (1980).

Major lines of action:

- tax concessions for conversion and replacement of oil/LPG equipment;

- subsidy for energy audits; awards for outstanding achievements;

- fuel economy goals for new cars (8 litre/100 km by 1987 - in 1983 actually 9.3 litre/100 km);

- graduated registration charges on vehicles based on weight or engine size;

- tax removed from ethanol fuel, all non oil heating appliances including solar;

- electrification of major railway lines; speed limits 60 km/hr in urban areas, 100 km/hr elsewhere;

- encouragement to automotive LPG: tax free and price kept at half of motor spirit;

- construction of 'low energy' houses;

- government programmes for the conversion of oil fired power plants.

CANADA

Supply

Canada is self sufficient in energy, its resources comprising coal, natural gas, hydropower, uranium and oil.

Exploration has a high success rate, particularly in the case of gas.

Future oil supplies are expected to come from existing oil regions in Alberta, the new oil sands projects and the frontier areas on the Canada Lands.

Gas requirements are expected to expand rapidly in the next decade. The main market for exported gas has been the United States, but LNG projects may open up markets in Europe and Japan.

Canada has changed from being a net coal importer in the 1970s to a net exporter in 1981. Constraints on the expansion of coal trade include high transport costs and the capacity of the rail system in a westerly direction. However, encouraging developments are taking place in the upgrading of the rail system and, in the longer term, in work on coal slurry pipelines.

Nuclear energy generation is based on the CANDU reactor system and has grown rapidly throughout the 1970s. Declining growth rates for electricity will reduce the demand for further nuclear energy.

Hydro electricity provided 69 per cent of Canada's total electricity production in 1981. Labrador and Quebec are areas of as yet undeveloped hydro resources.

Renewable energy sources, excluding hydro, are targeted to provide six per cent of TPE by 1990. Support is being given to the following:
- assistance to projects replacing petroleum products with peat and forest biomass;
- a programme to gain information on the operation of solar hot water heaters in Canada;
- projects for the production of synthetic gas from wood.

Demand/conservation
Efforts are being made to reduce oil consumption in the residential, commercial and industrial sectors. In the transport sector,

99

conversions to propane and Compressed Natural Gas vehicles are encouraged.

There are federal programmes for energy conservation in government establishments, retrofitting, propane vehicles (target: 8,000 vehicles by 1985), 'off oil' projects, industrial energy conservation, audits (with grants), energy research, forestry (20 per cent grant for projects replacing oil with peat, forest biomass and waste) with various considerable incentives (for example, 50 per cent contribution to the cost of approved energy efficient products or processes).

Voluntary fuel use level target for most cars: 8.6 1/km by 1985. Powerful propaganda for energy efficient driving.

Grants given for conversion of commercial and farm vehicles to propane (target: 100,000 by 1985), public car fleets to propane or CNG (target: 40 per cent by 1985) and other cars to CNG (30,000 by 1987). Up to C$50,000 contribution to retail refuelling outlets.

Conversion from oil to other fuels is supported by grants.

Energy labelling of major applicances is mandatory.

Conversion of oil fired power stations is promoted by major budgetary fund (mainly for the Atlantic provinces).

A state corporation is in charge of refinancing of conservation, renewable energy investments and some R & D (Canertech).

JAPAN

Supply

Japan is largely dependent on oil imports and is seeking to reduce this dependence through conservation measures and the development of alternative sources of energy.

Remarkable progress has been made in reducing the country's heavy dependence on oil, although net oil imports still represent over two thirds of total energy requirements. Some industries, such as iron and steel, are converting from oil to coal at a much faster rate than was anticipated. Crude oil imported in 1982 was down by almost 7 per cent over the previous year to 3.7 million b/d. The Sino-Japanese project to develop crude oil in China's Bahai Bay is to be speeded up. An agreement has been signed in 1983 with Saudi Arabia for a Japanese consortium headed by Mitsubishi to market over 80 per cent of methanol produced by the recently-opened Saudi Methanol Company.

Whilst domestic coal production is projected to decrease slightly in this decade, coal imports are expected to double. Some progress has been made to improve coal infrastructure.

Japan's nuclear generating capacity is planned to increase to 90,000 MW by the year 2000.

Hydropower, solar and geothermal systems have already reached the stage of practical use, while other new energy sources such as wind power and biomass are in the research and development phase. Magneto-hydrodynamic electricity generation is also one of the R & D projects.

The Japan Development Bank is concerned with long term investment in LNG, which is estimated to provide 11.6 per cent of total energy by 1990.

Demand/conservation

An active energy conservation policy is being pursued. Accelerated depreciation allowances are provided for newly purchased equipment with energy saving properties. Technical advice for small firms is offered by the Energy Conservation Centre. A large number of financial incentives is in operation for industry and also for residential/commercial buildings for example:

- 20-25 per cent reduction in local (property) tax for 3 years after acquisition of conservation equipment and concessional loans for financing it;

- subsidies for the commercialisation of 'alternative energy';

- subsidies for the improvement of public transport such as traffic engineering measures, new rail-feeder bus lines, etc.;

- premium loans for improving thermal efficiency in buildings and solar systems;

- subsidies and loans for improving intercity railways and construction of new 'town' railways.

Fuel efficiency in new cars is measured by a 10-mode test and sharp improvements are targeted. Speed limits: 40 to 100km/h.

NEW ZEALAND

Supply

New Zealand has been assessed as the fourth most energy rich country in the world on a per capita basis. Resources comprise hydro and geothermal power, natural gas and coal - with lignite deposits of 3,000 million tonnes. 90 per cent of total oil consumption is imported, mainly for the transport sector. Over the 1980s energy production is expected to almost double and self-sufficiency in energy will continue to increase to an expected 87 per cent by 1990.

Substantial coal reserves exist in New Zealand - lignite comprising 65 per cent of the present recoverable coal reserves. The discovery of lignite enables greater quantities of bituminous coking coals to be released to the international market.

Current oil reserves (25 mtoe) are mainly condensate. A detailed programme for the development of the McKee oil field has now been prepared and the field is expected to come on-stream by 1984.

With limited oil reserves, a key part of the energy policy is to capitalise on the vast reserves of the off-shore Maui gas field to achieve 50 per cent self sufficiency in transport fuels by 1987. Natural gas production is expected to increase fourfold. Condensate, a light oil found with Maui gas, will also become available. Eventually, about 10 per cent of New Zealand's cars will be fuelled by condensate.

Gas extraction facilities 'on-stream' from 1981 will eventually have a capacity of up to 130,000 tonnes of LPG a year, for use as a portable gas and as a transport fuel. A nationwide LPG supply system arising from new extraction facilities will place bulk depots at strategic points around the country.

The synthetic gasoline project developed by Mobil Oil provides for Maui gas to be converted into methanol and for a new process technology to turn methanol into high quality petrol.

Hydro-electric power accounts for 86 per cent of electricity generation.

Demand/conservation

The government's energy pricing policy has supported the substitution of imported oil with specific taxation and incentive schemes. The government operates an import parity pricing scheme and it seems likely that this will be extended to include synthetic gasoline.

The transport sector consumes 58 per cent of final oil consumption. Conservation measures in this sector include a standard driving test to monitor fuel efficiency in new vehicles; the encouragement of petrol saving devices; incentives to pool cars; and increased support for urban transport systems. The tax structure discourages the purchase of larger cars. A standard for vehicle exhaust emission testing is in preparation. New Zealand presently has three alternatives under development to displace imported oil in the transport sector: CNG, LPG and synthetic gasoline. All government vehicles (over 3000) have already been converted to CNG.

The bulk electricity tariff imposes an economic penalty for peak usage. This has encouraged local supply authorities to offer off-peak tariffs and ripple controls for domestic water heaters and storage space heaters. The government also has a loan scheme available for the installation of co-generation equipment.

There is a wide ranging system of financial incentives, including
- low interest loans for conservation and substitution with special payback criteria;
- 25 per cent grants for LPG storage;
- subsidies/loans for bus replacement and for certain bus operations;
- modernisation loan for suburban rail lines;
- grants for car conversion to CNG;
- 25 per cent grant (and in some cases a 100 per cent tax write-off)

and low interest loans for CNG filling stations;

- low interest loans for residential/commercial conservation;

- interest-free loans for solar water heaters.

Strict speed limits, with 80 km/h as the maximum.

UNITED STATES

Supply

Since the lifting of most earlier restrictions on oil and gas pricing, exploration for oil and gas has increased considerably. Only 40 per cent of oil imports to the USA now come from OPEC member countries, as reliance on other producers, such as Mexico and the North Sea has increased.

Natural gas production has increased. When completed, the Alaskan Natural Gas Transportation System (ANGTS) will link the lower 48 States with a major gas reserve.

Steam coal production represents the high growth area in coal output, and production is forecast to increase between now and 1995 at an annual average rate of growth of about 7 per cent. Future coal production is now considered to be limited largely by demand rather than supply constraints.

The expansion of the nuclear industry is hindered by poor public acceptability, technical problems and sharp increases in the cost of capital.

The earlier plans for and also the support given to synthetic fuels and producing oil from shales and tar sands have been partly reduced and partly postponed or (temporarily?) cancelled in view of the abundance of oil and its recently reduced basic price.

Demand/conservation

United States energy conservation policy, in the last two years, has placed stronger emphasis on the role of market forces in effecting desirable changes rather than specific government programmes.

Industrial energy consumption accounts for 32 per cent of TFC. Oil consumption in this sector has declined significantly.

The most substantial growth in demand in the residential/commercial sector is expected to be for electricity and renewable energy sources.

The government is stimulating demand for certain renewable energy sources through tax credits and regulatory incentives. Research is being carried out into developing advanced and commercial solar power systems and wind power (together with the continuing interest in further developing nuclear technology).

Mandatory fuel economy standards have reduced consumption in the transport sector: the 1985 target for new cars is 8.6 l/100km). A 'gas guzzler' tax has been imposed (started in 1980) on the sale of cars failing to meet standards. Speed limit overall: 88km/h.

Financial arrangements:
- energy tax credits to promote investment in modern plant;
- tax exemption on 'gasohol';
- various grants for low income people (owners and tenants) for energy saving, in some cases covering 100 per cent of costs of certain measures;
- tax credits for conservation in buildings (15 per cent of the first $2,000) and for renewable energy installations (40 per cent of first

$10,000);

- some solar installations are partly subsidised;

- grants for improved energy efficiency in schools and hospitals.

HUNGARY

Supply

Solid fuel is Hungary's major indigenous resource but the majority of production consists of brown coal and low quality lignite of which reserves are vast. This explains why the environmental protection policy concentrates heavily on the reduction of sulphur emission.

Only a small amount of crude oil is produced locally (about one fifth of consumption) and the remainder is imported, mainly from the USSR. Prices approximating the world price are being paid for Soviet oil, in roubles for a limited 'basic' quantity and in dollars (or other Western currency) for the excess. Hungary is connected to the Adria pipeline and could in principle, obtain Middle East oil via Yugoslav ports - but this pipeline has so far been hardly used.

Gas is popular; in the capital and major cities/towns where a gas distribution network exists it is mainly natural gas (about two thirds of domestic origin; the manufacture of town gas has been greatly reduced) and elsewhere bottled propane-butane.

The first nuclear station (with two reactors, altogether 1,000 MW) has come on stream (in 1984) and eventually will provide 20-25 per cent of requirements. Estimates (partly plans) foresee that by 2000 the contribution of oil/gas fired stations may be reduced to 20 per cent, that of coal stations increased, the present small hydropower (½ per cent) raised to 2½-3 per cent, and although imports may grow in absolute terms, their share should also decline.

107

Demand/conservation

Hungary's aim: to reduce the energy; GDP ratio from 1.1 in the early 1970s to 0.5. Technical development, structural changes, general and particular (though not outstanding) conservation measures should achieve this.

District heating is important in Budapest where a large part of dwellings and other premises (perhaps one third) is connected to networks based partly on hot springs and partly on CHP from local power stations.

Electricity requirements are planned to double in the twenty years to 2000. In 1980, about 40 per cent was generated by coal, a similar share by hydrocarbons and the rest, 20 per cent, was imported. The Hungarian national grid is connected with other CMEA countries and also with Austria and Yugoslavia.

YUGOSLAVIA

Supply

Yugoslavia is better endowed than most continental countries. Some two thirds of energy requirements are covered by domestic production of (low quality) solid fuel, hydroelectricity, limited quantities of oil and gas. Nevertheless, the country is reliant on imports of coking coal, crude oil and natural gas.

Unconventional forms of energy (such as geo-thermal energy, solar energy, waste materials) are planned to be used as of 1995 for supplying small scale consumers and as of 2000 for supplying industry.

Demand/conservation

Consumption of both solid fuel and natural gas is expected to increase in the next decade. However, consumption of coal (mostly brown coal and lignite) in its natural form will be reduced. Wood may be increasingly used.

A gradual reduction is expected in the use of both heating oil and gas oil in industry.

Electrical energy is expected, in the next decade, to satisfy a greater share of total energy requirements.

BRAZIL

Supply

The country is well endowed with resources but some of them are dislocated and far from consuming areas (eg hydro) or at present uneconomic (eg oil shale). Coal reserves are enormous but actual output covers no more than about one third of the modest usage; there are plans for trebling output. Geologically estimated oil possibilities are favourable, mainly onshore and exploration activity has been lively but at present oil production is small, covering perhaps 15 per cent of needs. One of the largest oil shale deposits is in Brazil and a pilot plant may start producing oil by 1985-6.

No more than about 15 per cent of the hydro potential is exploited; this supplies some 90 per cent of electricity. Significant further expansion is planned, partly jointly with neighbouring countries (such as, for example, the giant ITAIPO scheme on the Parana river, built by Brazil and Paraguay, with 12,600 MW eventual capacity).

No nuclear power is generated at present but the plans are for three stations (all PWR) by 1990, with a total capacity of 3,100 MW. Uranium reserves are quite considerable.

Among the newer types of fuel the most noteworthy is the alcohol programme. Based on sugarcane, the plan is to produce 10.7 billion litres by 1985 to replace gasoline. By then 20 per cent of all cars should run on alcohol and 80 per cent on a mixture of gasoline and up to one fifth alcohol.

Apart from research there is very little as yet in terms of solar or wind energy but some progress has been made in the diffusion of biogas in Sao Paolo State rural areas through better information and credit.

Firewood, timber and charcoal are also considered as replacements for oil and a significant reforestation programme was started around 1980.

Demand/conservation

Brazil is one of the very few countries with an official estimate of total energy consumption including non-commercial fuels. In 1979, renewable energy covered 55 per cent of domestic use (hydro 28%, firewood 17%, bagasse 5%, charcoal 3%, alcohol 2%) whilst non-renewables accounted for 45 per cent (oil 40%, coal $4\frac{1}{2}$%, gas $\frac{1}{2}$%). About 60 per cent of commercial energy - mainly oil - was imported (1981), absorbing about half of the country's total export earnings. This background explains the preoccupation with energy.

This preoccupation takes two main forms: the promotion of higher domestic production and conservation combined with the reduction of oil use.

Consumption of alcohol is at least 25 per cent higher than that of gasoline for the same performance but its price is being kept at a maximum 65 per cent of the gasoline price by a mandatory resolution.

In order to limit gasoline usage there is a low speed limit in force (80 km = 50 miles/hour) and the working hours of petrol stations are also limited.

Similarly, the price of coal, delivered to the consumer, "shall be at most 70 per cent of the lowest sales price per kilo-calorie of fuel oil".

There are large programmes under the supervision of an agency for identifying potential energy savings and allocating funds mainly for saving oil use (eg with a target of eliminating direct fuel oil use in the cement and steel industries by 1985).

COLOMBIA

Although Colombia is well endowed with all types of primary energy and has been self-supplying (and even a small net oil exporter in some years) ambitious plans are being implemented to expand coal production for raising internal use and also for exports.

Continued exploration has revealed major coal deposits in the eastern Andes mountains, estimated at 2,300 mtce (but this figure may be revised upwards) of which 1,800 mtce are at Cerrejon and are surface-mineable. In joint ventures the government is employing foreign capital and technology in order to double the present 6-8 million tonnes output in gradual steps to 12 million tonnes by 1985/6 and more than double again to over 30 million tonnes by 1990.

It is a characteristic feature of the development of coal (and other) mining in developing countries that almost half of the planned investment capital, some $3 billion for the Cerrejon project, is earmarked for infrastructural assets: $0.4 billion for connecting the mine to the port by rail and road; $0.4 billion for constructing the port; and $0.5 billion for building housing, airport and training facilities. Full production of 15-16 million tonnes should be reached in 1989; it is hoped to export most of it to Europe (in the belief that Colombian coal will be internationally competitive).

It is also forecast that domestic coal consumption, at present about one quarter of energy use, will be raised from the present 6-7 million tonnes to 15 million tonnes by 1990, about half of which will go to electric power generation.

EGYPT

Supply

Egypt is an oil exporter (but not a member of OPEC).

Exploration for oil and gas resulted in further commercial findings of both; several dry gas fields have also been found and a gathering pipeline system is under construction. Further expansion of hydropower is planned but this possibility is limited since two thirds of the Nile's potential is already being exploited. Coal deposits are not large; there are plans to exploit them in the future and also to start importing coal for power stations.

The use of solar power is still very limited, although the potential is great.

The most important item in the national plan is the building of nuclear power stations. The plans are spectacular: eight plants with a total capacity of nearly 8,000 MW which should provide some 40 per cent of the (probably over-estimated) demand for electricity by 2000. However, in view of the lower oil revenues, it is questionable whether the investment capital for this huge project will be available.

Demand/conservation

1981 energy use amounted to about 20 million tonnes oil equivalent: 3 mtoe non-commercial, 12½ mtoe oil, 1½ mtoe gas, about 1 mtoe coal and the rest hydropower. One fifth of the oil was used for thermal generation.

INDIA

Supply

Resources are modest. Coal reserves are large, oil and gas reserves small. Uranium reserves are limited but the hydro potential is large and only a small part is exploited; a good deal of the untapped potential is in the Himalayas where conditions are unfavourable.

Apart from oil, India is self-reliant, but oil imports weigh heavily on export earnings.

Stepping up the production of energy is planned by enlarging coal output (including new mines), a massive oil exploration and production programme and further hydro development, though this takes a long time. Nuclear capacity should be doubled by 1985 to 1.7 MW.

Land scarcity makes an alcohol programme virtually impossible but the setting up of (subsidised) biogas units is being encouraged, as well as small scale hydro generation. There are difficulties with non-commercial supplies; firewood is scarce and the forestry programme will hardly be able to balance the continued depletion; dung supplies are difficult to increase. This presents a social problem too since it hits the poor (80 per cent of household use in rural and 50 per cent in urban areas consists of non-commercial fuels).

A wide ranging R & D effort is being undertaken on solar and wind energy.

Demand/conservation

Wood, dung and agricultural waste account for about 45 per cent of total energy consumed in India; the quantities are staggering, estimated (1981/2) at 130 million tonnes of fuelwood, 70 million tonnes of dung and 40 million tonnes of waste. In 1981 commercial fuels used were, in million tonnes oil equivalent: 61 mt solid, 27 mt liquid, 2 mt gas and $4\frac{1}{2}$ mt primary electricity. In the same year, 58 per cent of electricity generated was thermal, 39 per cent hydro and $2\frac{1}{2}$ per cent nuclear.

The energy strategy emphasises the 'management of oil use' by various measures, such as a ban on oil or gas use at power stations; gradual electrification of Diesel railways and of Diesel-powered irrigation pump-sets; discouragement of long-haul road transport; financial support for the replacement of oilfired furnaces and boilers, etc.

Other measures, aimed more generally at conservation, include the encouragement of combined heat and power plants; improved irrigation pump sets; better wood (and kerosene) burning stoves, etc.

INDONESIA

Indonesia is a major exporter of oil and gas (mainly to Pacific countries). It is not surprising that the intention is to maintain these exports. Oil now accounts for 80 per cent of domestic use, gas for 18 per cent and coal and hydro for the remaining 2 per cent. The plans are to raise the non-oil contribution to 30 per cent by 1990. This is hoped to be achieved by the better exploitation of hydropower (at present hardly utilised) and geothermal energy, as well as coal. Reserves of the latter are estimated to exceed 10 billion tonnes whilst current production is under ½ million tonnes.

KENYA

Only about 30 per cent of energy use is commercial fuel, the rest locally collected fuelwood, etc. Oil accounted for 87 per cent of commercial energy, coal for 4 per cent (both imported, using up about one third of export earnings) and hydroelectricity for 9 per cent. Transport consumed 48 per cent and industry (mainly cement, food and oil refineries) another 33 per cent.

Rising prices have resulted in considerable initial conservation; hydro power and coal use have been growing slowly and solar water heating systems are spreading. The climate of Kenya is ideal for solar systems; their continued wider adoption represents great potential savings in oil and electricity for the future.

KOREA (SOUTH)

Of the 38 mtoe consumption of primary energy (1981) no more than about one quarter was home produced, consisting mainly of coal; the rest (23 mtoe oil and 5 mtoe coal) was imported. Apart from expensive coal, in difficult geological structures, and a small amount of nuclear and hydropower the country has no other energy resources.

Coal production is likely to decline and the plans are centered on two main objectives: building nuclear generating stations and importing coal. This should reduce dependence on oil (oil's share in primary energy use was 61 per cent in 1981). Nuclear plans should raise the present 560 MW capacity to 7,400 MW by 1990; in the same year coal imports - according to predictions - should reach 22-23 million tonnes, three times the present level.

The change can best be illustrated by the planned pattern of power generation. (1986 is based on the 10 year Power Development Program, 1990 on its likely continuation.)

	1981	1986	1990
Installed capacity MW	10,736	20,000	20,000
Fired by: *			
coal	12	15	21
oil	68	37	25
nuclear	5	32	41
other	15	16	13

*   in per cent of total fuel use.

SRI LANKA

In 1981, 60 per cent of energy consumed came from firewood and agricultural residues, 27 per cent from oil and 13 per cent from hydropower. Electricity use is limited, it serves perhaps 12 per cent of the households (1981) and less than one tenth of the villages. Thermal generation is small (turbines and diesels) and expansion of hydroelectricity is planned to dominate the future too. Four new hydro plants should be completed by 1986. These will make the further rural electrification possible.

With no resources at all except for hydro, the endeavour is being directed at replacing oil with imported coal and, mainly, forcing renewable types of energy. A UN programme has been set up to demonstrate that renewable sources can be harnessed to meet basic rural

116

needs. This includes a wind electric system (windmills coupled to generators); a solar electric system (based partly on thermal generator, partly on photovoltaic devices) and a biogas plant.

A re-afforestation programme has also been started.

THAILAND

Thailand used about 40 per cent of its export earnings in recent years to pay for the oil import bill. Oil accounts for 90 per cent of commercial (and about 75 per cent of total) energy use. It is planned to reduce its share in total energy to under 40 per cent by 1990. The main instruments to achieve this are the correction of inadequate pricing structures and the exploitation of domestic resources (gas, hydro, lignite) as well as coal importation.

In the twenty years to 1982 both the electric generating capacity and the road network increased by a factor of twelve. Energy production lagged behind. More recently, significant gas (on and offshore) and small onshore oil discoveries have been made; gas started to come on stream late in 1981. These, as well as lignite mining, are being expanded and six major hydro projects are being constructed, together with a number of mini-hydros in remote areas, for local needs.

Firewood and charcoal are estimated to contribute some 10 per cent to the energy supply; it is intended to balance deforestation by new plantings of fast-growing trees.

Biogas, wind, solar and oil shale are also mentioned in the plan, mainly as future possibilities.

WEST AFRICA

This section concerns the 16 countries that constitute the Economic

117

Community of West African States (ECOWAS).* It includes one major oil producer/exporter, Nigeria. Apart from Nigeria, Ghana, the Ivory Coast and Liberia, this is one of the poorest regions of the world.

Wood fuel dominates the energy pattern, accounting for almost 70 per cent of estimated usage (1979). The rest was mainly oil with the chief exception of hydropower which generated about half of the region's electricity, concentrated in Ghana, the Ivory Coast and Nigeria (very small hydro-generation exists in Guinea, Liberia, Mali, Niger and Togo). Nigeria alone used some gas and coal.

In view of the lack of an effective forestry programme the gradual scarcity of wood fuel seems unavoidable. Improved stoves would help greatly but few could buy them, even if cheap, without subsidy.

The river systems in the region provide huge hydro potential but only the four countries listed in the introductory paragraph above have the minimum level of power load which could justify the investment required by a major hydro plant; small schemes may be an option for others before a regional power network can be realised (perhaps in the next century).

Solar energy is an obvious possibility; some of the French speaking countries are actively pursuing it.

* Benin, Cape Verde, Gambia, Ghana, Guinea, Guinea-Bissau, Ivory Coast, Liberia, Mali, Mauritania, Niger, Nigeria, Senegal, Sierra Leone, Togo and Upper Volta

Notes

[1] Kouris, G, 'Oil trends and the prices in the decade: an aggregate analysis', <u>Energy Policy</u>, vol.12, no.3, September 1984.

[2] Morel, J, 'Real prices of energy', <u>National Institute Economic Review</u>, August 1980.

[3] 'Comparability' of course presents problems. Whilst these are all OECD countries (generally classified as industrial countries), there are nevertheless considerable differences between the structure of the UK economy and that of some others (for example, Denmark or Ireland). The residential sector has a much greater weight in energy use in Europe than in Japan where industry is a relatively larger consumer. Climatic differences can also play a part (for example, in Scandinavia).

[4] Johnson C, Denmark's energy policy, <u>Coal and Energy Quarterly</u> no 38, Autumn 1983.

[5] Summary of the Memorandum on Energy Policy, Ministry of Economic Affairs, The Hague, Part 1, September 1979, page 13.

[6] Dore, Ronald, Energy Conservation in Japanese Industry. Energy paper no.3, British Institutes' Joint Energy Policy Programme, Policy Studies Institute, London, 1982.

[7] Long,R, Coal in Japan's energy and economic development, <u>Coal and Energy Quarterly</u>, no.30, Winter 1983.

[8] There are other types of measures, partly compulsory, in the developing countries, concerning, for example, the introduction of improved stoves (West Africa and India) or irrigation pumps (India) but these are not relevant to UK conditions.

[9] For more details, see R. Dore, <u>op.cit</u>.

[10] This is a 'quango' founded in 1978; its budget is financed partly from the state budget (20 per cent), partly by private industry (35 per cent) and partly from the Bicycle Promotion Fund, a fund fed by revenues from the bicycle race betting tote (45 per cent).

[11] CNG = compressed natural gas; LPG = liquid petroleum gas.

[12] Energy policies and programmes of IEA countries, 1982 review, International Energy Agency, OECD-Paris, 1983, pp.391-2.

[13] Introduced by a Belgian energy group, developed in conjunction with a UK company. Financial Times, 27 March 1984.

[14] Report to the Secretary of State by the Combined Heat and Power Group chaired by Sir Walter Marshall, Energy Paper no 35, April 1979.

[15] W.S. Atkins and Partners, consulting engineers to the government, 1982.

[16] The House of Commons Select Committee on Energy, Third Report, 'Combined Heat and Power', April 1983.

[17] Peter Rost, MP, 25 February 1980, Hansard.

[18] Combined heat and power associated with district heating: a study of alternative schemes for Edinburgh and Glasgow, South of Scotland Electricity Board, May 1983.

[19] This estimate comes from the report of the International Energy Agency, Energy Policies and Programmes of IEA countries, 1983 Review, Paris, 1984, p.455, and is based on a scenario made by the Department of Energy for the 'Proof of Evidence for the Sizewell B Public Inquiry'.

[20] Various scenarios yield very different answers, depending, among other things, on the future price of oil and other conventional energy. In the most favourable conditions, for example, biofuels could contribute about 10 per cent of industrial heat demand by 2010; and 4.4 per cent of electricity could be generated by renewables, with a further possible contribution of 1.4 per cent from the Severn Tidal Barrage by 2025. Contribution of renewable energy technologies to future energy requirements, Energy Technology Support Unit (ETSU), Department of Energy, Paper No. ETSU R14, January 1983.